# SHE GREW ANYWAY

ASHLEY IRENE

**SHE GREW ANYWAY**

ASHLEY IRENE

First published by Ashley Irene 2026



First edition

Formatted with Vellum

Survival was the start. Becoming was the rest.

# CONTENTS

# DEDICATION

For the girl I once was, and for anyone who has ever carried a story like mine.

# AUTHOR'S NOTE

I did not begin writing this story from a place of certainty. I began with pieces of a life I had carried for years without fully understanding them. Some memories were sharp, others were blurred, and many lived quietly beneath the surface, shaping me long before I had the words to explain why.

For a long time, I believed that moving forward meant leaving everything behind. I tried to outrun the girl I used to be, the one who learned to survive by instinct and silence. But the past has a way of waiting for us, even when we think we have outgrown it.

Eventually, I reached a point where I could no longer pretend that distance was the same as healing. Writing this book became the way I finally allowed myself to look back — not to reopen wounds, but to understand the woman I became because of them. Every chapter is a step toward clarity, toward honesty, and toward the kind of strength that comes only after years of carrying what was never meant to be carried alone.

What follows is the truth as I lived it. It is imperfect, human, and shaped by the girl who held on and the woman who learned to rise.

*This is where my story begins.*

# PROLOGUE

I went back to the Midwest when my grandma fell ill. I hadn't planned on returning, not after everything that happened in that house and on that land. But something in me knew I needed to go home, to the place where my past waited in ways I hadn't faced.

Grandma's hospital bed sat in the middle of the living room, tucked near the couch. I sat beside her and sifted through a plastic bin of old photographs pulled from Uncle Lynn's closet. Dusty snapshots of a life I had almost convinced myself I imagined.

There was a little girl in those pictures. She wore a plastic princess crown and leaned over a birthday cake. A cousin sat beside her. My stepfather stood in the corner of the kitchen, steady and present, before everything between us shifted. I stared at those photos longer than I meant to. They felt like proof that once, things were simple. Safe. Steady.

Sitting beside that hospital bed, surrounded by pieces of a childhood I had spent years trying not to remember, I realized something. I needed to tell my story. Not for myself, but for the little girl in those pictures who had no idea how quickly steady could disappear.

Being back wasn't easy. The house was different, but the air felt the same. My step-grandpa moved quietly through the rooms, and my body reacted before my mind caught up. My shoulders tightened. My voice softened. My breath shortened. Memory lives in the body long after the mind tries to forget.

I didn't make it through the whole bin of photos. I didn't need to. I found enough. A girl who looked okay. Even happy. A girl who didn't yet know what she would have to carry.

I wondered when smiling turned into surviving.

If I could, I would wrap that little girl in my arms and tell her what no one told her then. There is light. You will be okay. You will build a life that feels nothing like this one.

But before that, you will learn how to leave. You will learn how to carry everything you own in your hands. You will learn that home can vanish overnight.

# THE WEEKEND THAT DIDN'T END

My mama dropped me off on a Friday and told me she'd be back Sunday. She always came back on Sundays. I'd stayed with Grandma Ann before, and I loved it because I got to play with my uncles and cousins. We were packed into that old trailer like beans in a can, barefoot, wild, loud. The rooms were too small, but somehow, we all fit.

That Friday felt no different than the others. Mama kissed the top of my head, said she loved me, and drove away in her car with the loud engine. I stood on the porch waving, watching the dust trail behind her.

I counted in my head the way I always did. One Mississippi. Two Mississippi. Until the car reached the end of the driveway and turned right.

Grandma Ann took care of all of us. Her bleached-blonde hair was always pulled back, her hands always busy, digging in the garden, stirring big pots on the stove, keeping us in line with just a look or by sending us to pick the greenest switch from a tree. Her green eyes saw everything, even when she wasn't looking right at you.

We lived on land in a small Midwest town. There were animals everywhere: chickens pecking, dogs barking, and a duck that once tried to eat my shoelace. I ran around barefoot until I stepped on a fire ant hill and learned real quick how fast those little things could bite.

It was crowded in that trailer. My uncles and cousins were close to my age, and we made our own kind of fun, hide-and-seek, mud pies, bumper cars, stick swords.

But even then, beneath the noise and movement, I felt it. The air would change before anyone said a word.

There were nights when quiet turned loud.

One night, my step-grandpa had been drinking. His words grew sharp and heavy, crashing into my grandma's voice. We kids were packed into the spare bedroom on old mattresses and piles of blankets, but none of us slept. We heard yelling. Things slamming. Grandma crying.

I pressed my hands over my ears, but the noise still got through.

Then sirens.

I crawled to the window and peeled back the blinds with my tiny fingers. Red and blue lights flashed across the yard. Men in uniforms walked up the porch, talking to my grandma, who held a towel to her face.

There was something dark on the towel. I stared at it too long.

I didn't understand everything, but I knew something bad had happened. And I knew Sunday wasn't coming the way I thought it would.

The next morning, the house felt different. Quiet in a way that made my chest feel heavy. Grandma Ann's face was swollen, one eye dark purple, and her lip split. But she didn't cry, not in front of us. She still made Malt-O-Meal. Still told

Uncle Ray to stop throwing things in the house. Still pulled on her boots and went out to feed the chickens.

But I saw it. I saw her hands tremble when she lit her cigarette. I saw her wince when she bent to pick up my uncle's toy. I saw the broken kitchen window, a jagged crack along the bottom pane, glass scattered across the counter like sharp, clear snow. A cool breeze pushed through it, carrying red dust from the yard.

It made the kitchen feel open. Exposed.

Nobody talked about what happened. Not the sirens. Not the yelling. Not the blood cleaned up before we woke. And nobody talked about where Mama went, either.

I asked once. "Grandma, when's Mama coming back?"

She paused, eyes not meeting mine. "She's figuring some things out, Irene."

Figuring what out? I wanted to ask. Did I do something? Is she mad? Did she forget?

I didn't know what that meant. But I stopped asking.

Days turned into weeks. I watched the long dirt driveway whenever a car pulled up. I waited for a knock.

Every time headlights turned in, my heart jumped so hard it hurt.

Eventually, waiting hurt more than not expecting, so I stopped.

Instead, I started helping more, picking tomatoes, standing beside Grandma in the kitchen, keeping my uncles and cousins from fighting. I learned to be useful.

If I was good enough, quiet enough, helpful enough, maybe someone would choose to keep me.

At night, I curled into my little blanket and whispered, "Good night, Mama," like maybe she could hear me wherever she was.

I said it softly. In case she was listening.

Uncle Ray and I were only a year apart, so I never called him "uncle." It didn't feel right. We were more like brother and sister. If I cried, he was usually the first one to sit beside me, even if he didn't say much.

That morning, after the sirens and the broken window, I found him out back by the driveway, dragging one of Grandma's kitchen spoons through the dry red dirt, carving another racetrack.

"You think she's coming back?" he asked without looking up.

I shrugged, crouching beside him. "She said she would."

He jabbed the spoon deeper into the dirt. "They always say stuff like that."

I didn't argue. I just hoped he was wrong.

We didn't talk after that. We just worked, shaping tracks, pouring water from mason jars, sending Hot Wheels flying down tiny hills.

Sometimes, if we were good at the grocery store, we were allowed to pick out one Hot Wheel each. They were ninety-nine cents. Ray always knew exactly which one he wanted. I always took forever. Choosing felt important — like the only moment that belonged just to me.

We got in trouble for stealing Grandma's spoons, but we didn't care. Playing made everything else go quiet: the yelling, the sirens, the ache in my chest.

Ray handed me his favorite Hot Wheel, a chipped red one with a missing wheel. "You can race with it today," he said. "It's the fastest."

Nobody had ever handed me something like that before. Not their favorite thing.

I didn't know what to say, so I nodded and lined it up at the top of the hill.

Secretly, that car stayed tucked in the pocket of my jean shorts for days. I'd reach in sometimes, feel the cool metal, and remember what it felt like to be just a kid.

For a moment, the waiting didn't feel so loud.

# THE RETURN

I was ten. Ray and I had been outside, covered in dirt, playing by the old yellow school bus that sat rusting in the tall grass. We had made it our clubhouse. Our hiding place. The sun was high. The cicadas screamed from the trees. For a moment, the world felt light.

Then I heard it.

"Irene! Irene!"

A black car came crawling up the gravel path, dust rising behind it like a ghost.

My heart jumped.

I froze. The kind of stillness that happens before your brain catches up.

I ran inside the trailer. "Grandma, who is that?"

She didn't look surprised. "It's your mom," she said.

The word landed hard.

Mom. Not Mama. Not Mommy. Just Mom. Like she had turned into someone else while I wasn't looking.

Months had turned into years.

She stepped out of the car like no time had passed. Tall. Thin. Familiar in a way that made my stomach twist.

"Get over here and see your Mama," she called.

Just like that.

I stood in the doorway, barefoot on the cool linoleum, my heart beating too fast.

My body moved toward her. The rest of me stayed behind.

I didn't know what her return meant.

Was I in trouble? Was I going with her? Was she going to leave again?

She wrapped her arms around me, and I let her.

She smelled like smoke and something sweet I couldn't name. My arms stayed stiff at my sides for a second too long before I made them hug back.

I counted without meaning to.

But part of me stayed in the doorway.

I watched my grandma's face, trying to read it. I never really could. She stayed calm. Too calm.

Her mouth was tight. Like she was biting down on something she wasn't going to say.

My mom didn't come inside. She stayed on the porch my step-grandpa had built, standing like she had never left.

Then I stepped outside.

"I've been back," she said. "I'm living with a friend now. Got a little apartment. I'm working. I'd like you to come stay with me on some weekends."

I lowered my eyes and nodded.

I didn't ask the questions pressing against my chest.

Where were you? Why didn't you come get me sooner? Did you miss me?

She smiled like it was good news. Like this was something to celebrate.

Friday afternoon came quickly. School ended, and she was already there, standing near the porch. Her long blonde hair looked lighter than I remembered. A cigarette rested between her fingers. She waved like we had just seen each other yesterday.

I walked toward the car slowly, my backpack heavy on one shoulder.

I didn't know if I was supposed to feel excited. Or careful.

"There's my girl," she said, reaching over to mess up my hair.

It felt familiar. And not.

She asked if I was hungry. I was. At Grandma's, there were too many kids and not much money. On rare days, we shared ninety-nine-cent Whoppers like they were something special. And to me, they were.

That day, she took me to Taco Bell.

I stared at the menu too long, overwhelmed by the choices.

There were so many options. I didn't want to choose wrong. I didn't want to cost too much.

She ordered for me. A bean burrito with hot sauce.

We ate in the car. I took careful bites, holding the wrapper tight so nothing spilled.

I kept my elbows tucked in, careful not to make a mess.

She talked easily, like this was already routine. I listened more than I spoke.

When we reached the apartment, her friend opened the door and smiled.

"So this is the famous daughter," she said.

My chest tightened.

Famous for what? For being left? For being the kid who stayed behind?

The apartment smelled like cigarette smoke and old carpet. Not dirty. Just heavy. Mail stacked on the counter. An ashtray crowded with lipstick-stained cigarette butts.

I stood near the door, unsure what to do. My mom moved through the space like it was hers.

I followed behind her.

Not like a daughter. More like someone who was visiting.

She showed me where I would sleep. Not really a bedroom. Just a den with a futon on the floor and a fleece blanket folded neatly on top. Pink. Soft.

She sat down and patted the spot beside her.

"So," she said. "What's new with you?"

I shrugged.

How do you explain years in one sentence?

That weekend, people came and went. Friends, she said. Some had kids. I stayed quiet, sitting on the floor, watching. Something about it made my stomach tighten.

The way the adults laughed too loud. The way the air felt thick. The way bottles appeared without anyone saying they were drinking.

I kept track of the door.

At my grandma's, we learned to leave when the drinking started. No explanations. Just go. I didn't tell my mom about those nights.

I kept those stories packed away.

If I told her, it might ruin this. And I had just gotten her back.

That weekend was the start of something new and complicated.

I thought getting her back meant everything would feel better. Instead, it felt like learning a new set of rules.

I watched and tried to memorize them.

*Only that nothing would ever be simple again.*

# THE PULL BETWEEN TWO WORLDS

In the beginning, weekend visits with my mom were consistent. She picked me up. We ate together. We spent time side by side. It felt like she was trying. Like she wanted to prove she was back.

She felt familiar. But still new.

Then she started dating.

He was different.

I didn't have a word for what he was. I only knew my stomach tightened when he walked into the room.

The air changed when he was around. My mom's shoulders drew in. Her laughter sounded smaller.

She watched his face before she answered questions.

Her attention fractured. The woman who had stood tall on the porch that first day began to disappear in pieces.

Her friends were a mix. Some were kind. They cheered her on. Told her she deserved a fresh start. Others brought noise with them. Loud music. Louder voices. Bottles that emptied quickly.

One night, a man broke into her apartment and hid behind

the door.

I remember the sound before I understood what it was.

A thud. Then shouting. My heart pounding so hard I could hear it in my ears.

I remember the door swinging open.

I remember a shape in the dark.

After he was gone, no one explained much.

I slept with the light on for weeks during our visits.

Life didn't get easier at my grandma's house either. The drinking came and went like weather you could not predict. My step-grandpa had a way of shrinking rooms.

He called me "slave."

The first time he said it, I froze.

No one laughed.

He barked orders while he cooked steak and cubed potatoes in a greasy skillet that filled the kitchen with a thick smell. He never cooked for us kids. Just himself.

If I asked to sleep over at a friend's house, his face hardened.

"Who's gonna clean the house if you're gone?"

The words stayed with me.

I started asking less.

I asked my grandma anyway. Sometimes she said yes.

Those nights felt like oxygen. Clean sheets. Quiet kitchens. Parents who tucked their kids in and meant it.

But coming home always carried a cost.

Silence. Sharp words. Chores stacked higher than before.

As I grew older, something shifted. Not just with him, but with my grandma too.

Her warmth toward me cooled.

She still fed me. Still kept a roof over my head. But something in her eyes pulled back.

She stopped reaching for me first.

I couldn't tell if it was fear. Exhaustion. Or something else entirely.

Maybe loving me felt like choosing sides. Maybe I was afraid of that, too.

Sometimes my mom came to get me in the middle of the night. No warning. Just headlights sweeping across the yard. Gravel crunching.

A police officer stood beside her.

No explanation.

"Come on. You're coming with me."

I would stand there in pajamas, hair messy, heart racing.

No one asked what I wanted.

She took me to unfamiliar places to sleep. Couches. Apartments I did not recognize. Rooms that smelled different.

Then she brought me back the next morning.

Too late for the school bus.

No one asked questions.

That back and forth became my normal.

Never fully settled in either place.

Never fully claimed.

I learned how to pack lightly.

A toothbrush. A change of clothes.

*Nothing I loved too much.*

*Nothing I couldn't carry myself.*

# A SHIFT IN THE AIR

The trailer was different from the apartment. It sat still and quiet most days, like it was holding its breath.

My mom was juggling work and relationships, and whatever else filled her hours. I began to notice small things.

The way the trailer park felt heavy in a way I couldn't name. Like the air clung to your skin. Like everyone knew something about everyone else, and no one said it out loud.

I was twelve. Just starting middle school. But I felt older than most of the kids around me.

I didn't rush anymore.

I didn't feel like a kid who got to just be loud and careless. I felt like someone who needed to know what was happening before it happened.

I watched more than I spoke. I learned to read rooms before I entered them. I stayed quiet.

But I was always paying attention.

My mom talked about fresh starts. About making things better. I listened carefully.

Hope felt expensive. I wasn't sure we could afford it.

Sometimes things felt good for a while. Then they didn't.

I wasn't angry.

I just stopped expecting things to last.

I stopped waiting for my life to return to something normal and began to understand that this was my normal. Moving between homes. Shifting between versions of myself. Adapting to what each place required.

I learned which parts of me belonged where.

At twelve, something inside me hardened.

And sharpened.

I learned how to shrink myself in one house and expand in another.

I could see my mom was trying the best way she knew how. She had energy. Big ideas. A restless spirit. She bought me things sometimes. Took me out to eat. Tried to squeeze years of missed memories into a weekend.

She planned little adventures. Things I never got to do at my grandma's house.

I appreciated them.

I really did.

But there was a quiet guilt I couldn't name.

If I laughed too hard, it felt like betrayal. If I missed her, it felt dangerous.

I lived between two versions of myself, never fully settling into either one.

Most weekends, when I stayed with her, I was alone in the trailer. She worked long hours. Sometimes late into the night.

I slept on the futon in the living room.

Occasionally, a boyfriend would come around. She was careful. Protective in ways that felt deliberate.

I could tell she was trying to do something different than before. Trying to keep me out of it.

One night, I woke to knocking.

Sharp. Urgent.

Not polite.

My eyes snapped open. The trailer felt small. I watched my mom walk to the door.

Two men stepped inside.

I didn't move.

I stared at the wall and held my breath, counting silently, waiting for yelling. Waiting for something to break.

They spoke in low voices.

I squeezed my eyes shut.

When I woke up in the morning, they were gone.

No one mentioned it.

There were good moments too.

Soft ones.

The trailer park had a pool. We spent long afternoons there in the heat. My mom poured lemon juice into my hair, hoping the sun would streak it blonde. She lay on a towel listening to music while I jumped in and out of the water, trying to make her laugh.

When she laughed, I felt chosen.

For a little while, everything else faded.

As summer drifted into fall, I felt another shift. I was still living with my grandma full-time. Still catching the bus from her house every morning.

School gave me structure when everything else felt uncertain.

At school, I blended in.

Inside, I carried a quiet weight.

I paid closer attention to my mom's voice on the phone. The way she sometimes sounded tired. Distracted.

The way she sounded like she was trying to convince herself that everything was okay.

I noticed how she smiled through the worry in her eyes when she picked me up. How hard she tried to make weekends feel like celebrations.

As the air grew colder, the pool visits faded.

I sensed we were both clinging to summer.

My mom went through moments of joy.

I learned to rise and fall with them.

We didn't talk about feelings. Or the past.

But I knew she loved me.

I felt it in the small gestures. The way she tucked a blanket around me on the futon. The way she saved the last bite of something she knew I liked.

That love felt different from the love at my grandma's house.

Not better. Not worse.

Just different.

At Grandma's, love felt like survival. At my mom's, love felt like trying.

Around that time, I met Molly.

She lived a few trailers down.

At first, we just waved. Then one afternoon, she asked if I wanted to come over.

That small question changed everything.

Molly had an easy laugh. She didn't study me the way I studied people. Her trailer house wasn't bigger or nicer, but it was full. Noise. Movement. Siblings running in and out. Her mom calling out from the kitchen.

There was always someone home.

I didn't realize how much that mattered until I felt it.

I spent more time there. Soaking in the warmth of that noise. When we weren't inside, we were outside, daring each other to do stupid things. Wandered to the edge of the property where the fence met the woods.

Molly made the weekends lighter.

She filled the quiet spaces I didn't know how to name.

Then I started my period.

I was at Molly's trailer, watching TV. My mom wasn't home.

We had never talked about this.

When I saw the blood, panic took over.

I thought I was hurt. I thought something inside me had broken.

I locked myself in Molly's bathroom.

The room felt too small. The light too bright.

I stared at my underwear like it was a crime scene.

I didn't know what was happening.

Only that something had changed.

And I was alone in it.

Molly's mom knocked gently.

"It's okay," she said.

Her voice was calm. Steady.

She handed me an old-fashioned pad that clipped into my underwear. It felt bulky. Strange.

I felt embarrassed—grown and little at the same time.

When I finally told my mom, she didn't sit me down for a serious talk.

She filled a cup with water.

Dropped a tampon into it.

We watched it swell and expand.

Then she lifted it out and started swinging it by the string, laughing.

"This is what happens inside you," she said.

It was strange.

A little funny.

Completely her.

That was how she told me I had become a woman.

Unfiltered.

Honest.

Imperfect.

And somehow, even in that awkwardness, I felt her trying to give me something she *never* got herself.

# THE OTHER SIDE OF HOME

Living at my grandma's trailer was a different kind of quiet. Not empty, just settled. The hum of the heater in the morning. The tap of her spoon against her coffee mug. The TV flickering with the morning news. Every day followed the same pattern. Wake up. School. Come home. Dinner. Sleep. Nothing surprised me there.

I did not have my own room, but I had a place—a twin bunk bed in the corner. My backpack stayed tucked beside it. I kept my things close. That small space felt important.

Breakfast was Malt-O-Meal at the tiny kitchen table, steam rising while I stirred in sugar. Grandma did not hover. She did not ask many questions. She folded laundry, rinsed dishes, and moved through her routines without much noise. The trailer was not fancy, but it was warm and clean. It felt steady.

Most of my clothes were hand-me-downs from my cousin. Slightly worn. Sometimes out of season. After I started my period, there was a new rule. When I came home from school, I changed into something loose. Something modest. No explanation. I followed it.

I began folding my arms across my chest without thinking. I walked through rooms quickly. I kept my eyes down.

Grandma's care showed up in hot meals and clean laundry. In rules. Do not stand out. Do not draw attention. Blend in. Be small.

At school, girls wore bright shirts that fit close to their bodies. They laughed loudly in the hallway. I layered my clothes and kept moving.

The trailer felt temporary. Thin walls. A roof that shook during storms. I learned how to close doors without letting them click. How to step lightly across the floor. How to disappear into a corner if I needed to.

Stephanie came into my life in sixth grade. I was on crutches after falling down the trailer stairs at Molly's place. I hated the way everyone stared at the metal and rubber under my arms. I got to go to lunch early so I would not get knocked over in the hallway.

That is when Stephanie tripped me.

On purpose.

My crutches slid out from under me and clattered across the tile. My face burned. I wanted the floor to open up and swallow me.

We both ended up in the school counselor's office. The plan was simple. Sit together for a week and work on getting along, and no arguing. No talking back. Just quiet worksheets at the same table.

We talked anyway.

First, out of boredom. Then, because we liked the same music. The same jokes. By Friday, we were laughing so hard the counselor had to separate us again.

That fall turned into something else.

Stephanie saw me. I did not have to measure every word around her.

I started asking to sleep over at her house. Her home felt loud in a good way. Movies playing in the background. Bread with cheese and ranch. Staying up too late and whispering under blankets.

I was only allowed one night.

Because of him.

If I was not home, it became a problem. I was expected to be there. Ready to clean. Ready to help. Ready when my name was called.

His hugs lasted too long. When he said, "Come here," I went. I felt like I didn't have a choice. I kept my arms straight at my sides. I stared at the wall behind him and counted in my head. Holding still felt like the only control I had.

Sometimes I called Grandma and asked to stay another night at Stephanie's. Sometimes she said yes. Sometimes it did not matter. He would show up anyway. A tight grip on my arm or my hair. Silence in the truck on the way back.

I watched the houses pass through the window and blinked hard so I would not cry. I pressed my fingernails into my palm until they left half-moon marks.

If I stepped out of sight for too long at home, he would yell. My name sounded sharper when he said it. Like I had done something wrong just by being somewhere else.

That house always felt tense, like the walls leaned in.

At Stephanie's, I could breathe.

I tried to tell her once.

We were flipping through a teen magazine, circling outfits with a glitter pen. Her room was messy in a way that felt alive. Posters peeling at the corners. Clothes tossed across a chair.

"Do you ever have to clean the walls at your house?" I asked.

She looked at me. "The walls?"

"Like wipe them down. Or you get yelled at."

She frowned. "No. Just my room."

I nodded like it was normal. My throat burned.

At home, he dragged his fingers across the paneling, checking for dust that was not there. If he found any, he called me lazy. Then he told me to come here. Like it was forgiveness.

His hands did not stay where they should. They never did. I held my breath and counted.

I did not tell Stephanie all of that. Not yet. She set the magazine down and asked if I wanted to sleep over again.

I said yes, even though I already felt the knot in my stomach about going back.

Life moved between three places then. Grandma's trailer. Stephanie's house. And my mom's trailer, where nothing ever stayed in the same place for long.

With my mom, I tried to guess who she wanted me to be. When music came on, she changed. Jewel. Alanis. Sarah McLachlan. She closed her eyes and sang like she was somewhere else.

Sometimes a man came over. Sometimes I tried to keep the trailer clean, like maybe order would make everything feel safer. There was a spare room in the back, piled with my mom's extra things — boxes, clothes, old blankets, stuff she didn't have space for. I wanted a room of my own so badly that one afternoon, I started dragging everything into trash bags, stacking them in the corner to hold up the mattress that sat on the floor. For a moment, it looked almost like a real bed. Almost like a room that could belong to me.

She worked at a place where she danced. I did not know what that meant. I only knew her dresser was full of sparkly clothes. When she was gone, I tried them on. I spun in front of the mirror and studied myself. Then I folded everything back exactly the way I found it.

No matter how bright the sparkly clothes were, the spare

room still felt crowded — like it belonged to everyone and no one at the same time.

Sometimes I broke rules just to feel something different.

I found a stray dog once and hid it in the spare room. I fed it scraps and whispered secrets into its fur. It felt good to take care of something.

Another time, I took the car. The keys were on the counter. I drove slowly around the trailer park, hands tight on the steering wheel. My heart pounded so hard I thought it might give me away. I hit a curb and scraped the tire. When my mom asked what happened, I lied. She did not ask again.

Sometimes I called a cab and went to the mall. I walked through stores like I belonged there. I stood in the food court and watched other families eat together.

For a little while, I pretended.

And when everything went quiet again, I lay awake, staring at the ceiling, holding questions I did not know how to ask.

# THE FAMILIAR RHYTHM

Back at Grandma's, nothing really changed, and that was the point.

I went to school. I did my chores. I followed the rules. Days passed without calling attention to themselves, and I learned how to move through them quietly.

My mornings followed the same order every day. Wake up early. Eat a quick breakfast. Grab my backpack. Head out the door. The bus ride was predictable, filled with the usual chatter and giggles of classmates who didn't know how much silence could live inside a house.

Grandma's house wasn't a home in the way other kids described theirs, but it held me in place while I figured out how to exist there. The TV was always on. Something was always cooking. Knick-knacks crowded the shelves, books stacked wherever they fit. Everything stayed the same, even as I learned how to adjust myself to it.

At school, I sat with Stephanie. Our friendship had grown from that clumsy moment in the lunch line, and somehow she became the person I talked to the most. We claimed a corner table and filled the time with jokes and stories, circling around everything except the things that felt too heavy to name.

With her, I didn't have to explain myself. She didn't ask questions I wasn't ready to answer. For a little while each day, I could forget what waited for me after the last bell.

School itself stayed steady. I blended in. I kept my head down. I moved through lessons without drawing attention. Other kids talked about plans, about home, about weekends that stretched ahead of them. I had my books, my routines, and Stephanie. I learned early that life worked best when I stayed predictable and out of the way.

It wasn't peace. It was survival disguised as routine.

# SAFE SPACE

The world around me felt unpredictable and full of chaos, but there was one place where I could breathe. One place where I didn't have to worry about being someone I wasn't, where I could exist without bracing myself.

That place was Lisa's office.

She was the school counselor and the only adult at school who seemed to notice how much I was carrying.

I started seeing her regularly, and each visit felt like a pause. A brief place to land away from everything that felt unsteady at home. Her office was small. Two chairs. A shelf of books. A basket of stress balls and worn-out board games. Nothing fancy. Just quiet.

The door closed softly when I walked in. That sound felt like permission to let my shoulders drop.

I didn't have to pretend there. I didn't have to perform.

I often sat quietly, unsure of where to begin. Lisa never rushed me. She didn't fill the silence. Sometimes she would just lean back in her chair and wait. Sometimes she handed me a piece of paper and a pen and let me draw instead of talk.

If I wanted to talk about my mom, I did. If I didn't, that was okay too.

No one had ever let me choose like that before.

I shared the things I could say without my throat tightening. I told her about my mom's drinking. About the loud music. About how weekends sometimes felt long and strange.

I stayed near the edges.

I didn't tell her about the counting. Or the dust checks. Or the way my shoulders rose when certain footsteps came down the hallway.

Still, what I said was enough for her to understand I needed help.

I didn't tell her everything. I still believed that some things were better left unsaid.

But I began to notice something.

When I left her office, my chest felt lighter.

I wasn't fixed. I was simply no longer carrying everything alone.

Lisa never pushed me to say more than I could. She let me take my time.

In that patience, she showed me something new.

That adults could be steady.

She was the first person who made me feel like I could sit in a room without shrinking.

I carried those quiet visits with me long after I left her office. They became proof that places like that could exist.

Proof that maybe I wasn't invisible.

And somewhere inside me, a small part began to believe I might one day build a room like that for someone else.

# CHANGING ENVIRONMENTS

One weekend, my mom told me she would move closer to my school and closer to my friend Stephanie if I came to live with her. I wanted to get away from my step-grandpa. I could feel his eyes lingering where they weren't supposed to, and he had started coming into the room where I slept late at night.

But I loved my grandma. I loved my uncles. And in that house, I had known moments of comfort. Parts of it felt like home, and when my step-grandpa wasn't around, I felt safe there.

Leaving would mean leaving them. Not forever, but it felt permanent to my middle school heart. I was being asked to choose between the people I loved and the safety I needed.

I carried that guilt quietly. I didn't know how to explain why I was considering moving in with my mom, or how complicated the decision really was. My grandma wasn't happy. She didn't fight me on it, but her disappointment lived in the room.

"I knew this day would come," she said.

There was no long goodbye. No lingering hug. Just the

silence that settles in when someone's heart is breaking and they don't have the words, or the power, to stop you from leaving.

I moved in with my mom in seventh grade.

I didn't know what it would be like. My young mind held onto the good things. Being closer to Stephanie. A place that felt new. The idea that maybe this was a fresh start. I didn't think about what else could happen. I didn't think about the weight of living with someone who, even though she was my mom, still felt like a stranger in many ways.

The apartment was just down the street from Stephanie's home, and I couldn't believe how happy that made me. We didn't have cell phones then, but there was a payphone in the apartment complex, and we thought it was the greatest thing.

We called our friends, made plans, or just talked until we ran out of change, which happened all the time. Then we dug through couch cushions and laundry piles for quarters like it was a treasure hunt.

At first, it felt like freedom. Like my life was finally shifting.

But my mom worked late into the night, sometimes not coming home until morning. Sometimes not at all. She told me she was doing it for us. And maybe she was. But when you're thirteen, and the apartment is dark, and the only sound is the clock ticking, explanations don't quite quell the loneliness.

They don't fill the space where a parent should be.

That first taste of freedom came wrapped in a quiet isolation, one that taught me early how to be alone, even when I wasn't far from the people I loved.

I thought the move would change everything. I didn't know it was only the beginning of a different kind of struggle.

# THE OTHER SIDE

I believed that leaving the house where my step-grandpa's eyes were always on me would solve everything. I told myself distance would equal safety. I pictured a fresh start, a life where I could finally exhale. But some struggles don't end just because the address changes.

The apartment was fine. Close to friends. Close to school. But it held a different kind of heaviness. My mom wasn't there most nights. The silence stretched long after dark, broken only by the hum of appliances or the sound of my own thoughts. Some of them were comforting. Others weren't.

Stephanie and I roamed the apartment complex like we owned it. We laughed too loudly, lingered outside too late, and sometimes got into trouble. Those moments felt like borrowed freedom.

Before I left, I wrote notes for my mom in case she came home while I was gone.

"Gone to Stephanie's. Be back soon."

Those notes were my way of pretending we were still

connected. A small attempt to anchor myself to someone who wasn't there. A way of saying, "I'm here," even when she wasn't.

My mom started dating a guy in the Navy. He seemed nice. Confident. Charming. He brought gifts, took us out to eat, and sometimes we went to his house. For a while, I let myself believe this one might stay. My mom had a way of pulling people in, and I wanted to believe that meant stability.

After a few months, something shifted.

We were on our way to Six Flags with a friend when everything turned. I still don't understand what set it off, but suddenly he pulled the car over and kicked us out. The excitement vanished, replaced by yelling that filled the air, anger colliding with fear where laughter had been moments before.

That was the first time I understood how quickly things could turn. How warmth could disappear without warning. I learned when to speak and when silence was safer. I learned how to make myself smaller. I learned the shape of a room when someone's mood could change without reason.

My mom had been in bad relationships before. This time, I was living inside one.

And I couldn't leave.

My mom was strong. She stood her ground. Fear didn't seem to live in her. But it lived in me. I felt it settle in my stomach whenever those men were around, a quiet warning I couldn't ignore.

Something always happened. Yelling. Shouting. Then the silence afterward, sharp and cold.

The Navy guy apologized to me sometimes. His voice would soften. His eyes would fill with tears. He brought small gifts, peace offerings meant to smooth things over. And for a while, things would be calm. A day. Maybe a week.

But the pattern never changed.

The calm never lasted. The yelling returned. The silences followed. And the weight in my chest grew heavier each time.

I was learning a truth I didn't have words for yet: you can escape a place, but not a pattern.

I was trapped inside a cycle I didn't create and didn't know how to escape.

# SOMEWHERE TO BREATHE

When it was too loud at home, too tense, too confusing, I went to the places where I could breathe. Lisa's office, the school counselor's space, was one of them. I didn't need an appointment or permission. I never asked to go. She was simply there, part of the building, part of my days.

Lisa's office hadn't changed. Same two chairs. Same quiet kindness. Sometimes I didn't need to speak at all. Just sitting in that room reminded me that I existed, that I took up space in the world.

I hadn't been there regularly for a while, not since things shifted at home, but she still noticed me. She always seemed to check in at the right moment, like she could sense when things were starting to close in.

Stephanie's house became more than a place to hang out. It became a landing spot when home felt too tight. Her mom welcomed me with soft eyes and open arms. I never explained why I was there so often, and I don't think I needed to. Some adults understand without being told.

At her house, I didn't have to stay alert. No pressure. No careful listening for changes in tone or mood. Just laughter, late-night talks, and plans that didn't always work out. It felt uncomplicated in a way my life rarely was.

One morning, I walked to her house early so we could catch the bus together. When we missed it, we didn't tell anyone. We set out for school in flip-flops, two girls pretending the day belonged to us. Our feet were soaked from the morning dew, grass clippings sticking to our skin, but even when our legs ached, we laughed the whole way.

We were late. But we made it.

And for once, being late didn't feel like failure. It felt like choosing ourselves. A small rebellion in a world we didn't control.

We walked into the school office, damp and out of breath, and said, "We missed the bus."

They sent us to class. That was it. No questions. No concern. No one looked too closely.

Later that afternoon, Lisa stopped by my classroom. She smiled, leaned against the doorway, and said, "I just wanted to check in."

I didn't tell her everything. I didn't have to. She knew how to listen without prying. Sometimes being seen was enough.

Since moving in with my mom, I'd grown quieter. More guarded. I learned quickly that saying the wrong thing could make life harder, not better. Real consequences, not just raised voices or rules. So I held my words close, and Lisa understood that.

I didn't need to explain myself.

She just wanted me to know I hadn't disappeared.

# ALMOST ENOUGH

Despite everything, I was doing better than ever at school. For the first time in my life, I made the Honor Roll. My name would be announced at an assembly, and my mom said she would be there. I laid my clothes out the night before, lining everything up just right, folding them carefully on the edge of the bed my mom and I shared.

That morning, the apartment was quiet. No movement. No sound. No sign of her.

I got dressed slowly, half-expecting to hear her footsteps at any second. My stomach twisted as I tied my shoes. Every small sound felt louder in the stillness.

At school, I sat in the gym while names were called. I watched kids scan the bleachers, searching for faces they knew. I searched too, row by row, face by face. She wasn't there.

I told myself she probably forgot. I told myself not to make it into something bigger. But a familiar fear whispered that she might have left.

On the bus ride home, I stared out the window, willing time to move differently. The apartment was empty when I got there.

I sat for a while, not angry, just tired. Hollow. Then I heard the door.

My mom walked in, and something was immediately wrong. A brace wrapped around her neck. Her arm held in a sling.

She told me she and her Navy boyfriend had been arguing in the car. He had driven them into an underpass wall on the highway.

I didn't know what to say. There were no words that made sense. I wanted to be angry. I wanted to ask why she hadn't been at the assembly. I wanted her to care about my name being called. To really see me, just this once.

Instead, I nodded and helped her settle in. That was the role I knew how to play.

I made her eggs, using too much oil until they slid around the pan. I carried the plate slowly back to our room, concentrating so they wouldn't spill. She ate them without a word.

Honestly, I'm not sure I would have.

She slept most of the day. The apartment stayed quiet. I felt safer knowing exactly where she was — not because she was okay, but because I didn't have to wonder. Safe because I didn't have to imagine what might have happened this time.

She was still my mom.

And I still loved her.

# JUST KEEP GOING

The hurt, the letdown, they dulled with time, not because they healed, but because I learned how to carry them. Day by day, my mom recovered, and life slid back into familiar patterns. I kept moving forward, because that was all I knew how to do. One foot in front of the other. Just keep going.

She was still with the Navy guy, still unpredictable. But I went to school, hung out with Stephanie, laughed with friends, and did what I could to feel normal. Even the hum of fluorescent lights at school felt calmer than the apartment. Even the smell of cafeteria food felt steady.

I blended in as best I could, a middle schooler clinging to small certainties, holding onto anything that made life feel manageable, even if it was something as simple as walking to the store with friends or feeding quarters into the payphone at the apartment complex.

There were days when I thought things might stay calm. Days when I almost forgot to stay guarded. Then one afternoon after school, Stephanie and I were outside the apartment door, messing around with a skateboard. We had no idea how to ollie, but that didn't stop us from trying. We laughed, half falling, pretending we were one jump away from nailing it, until the board flew out from under us and slammed into the neighbor's door.

My stomach dropped. My heart hammered. That familiar rush of panic flooded my chest.

The door swung open. A woman stood there, furious.

We tripped over our apologies, both blurting out "Sorry!" at the same time.

She didn't say much. She just looked at us like we were the final straw. Her stare lingered longer than her words, heavy and unforgiving.

The next day, when I got home from school, an eviction notice was taped to our apartment door.

My heart raced. I didn't know what to do, so I shoved it into the bottom of my backpack, under my notebooks, as if hiding it could erase it, or at least delay the fallout. The stiff paper pressed against my ribs like a warning I couldn't escape.

It wasn't the smartest choice, but it was the only control I felt I had. I told myself it couldn't be just the skateboard. What about the loud music late at night, Jewel, Alanis Morissette, and Sarah McLachlan echoing through the walls? What about the slammed doors, the yelling, the arguments?

It takes more than one warning to evict someone… right?

When my mom found the eviction notice, going through my backpack while I wasn't home, she exploded. She yelled about the skateboard, about everything suddenly at risk. Then she started throwing things, whatever was closest. A cup. A book. The remote. One object shattered against the wall. Another tipped over a lamp. The crashes made my stomach flip, my hands shake, my chest tighten.

I stood there frozen.

My mom never learned how to pause before reacting. Her childhood hadn't protected her the way it should have. It hadn't taught her how to love gently or steadily. She lived in fight-or-flight mode, and most days, she chose fight.

I took it personally. I thought if I hadn't hidden the notice, if I'd said the right thing, been quieter, easier, less.

Even then, some part of me understood this wasn't really about me.

Her reactions came from places I couldn't see: old wounds, unresolved fear, patterns passed down without warning. I felt the blast without ever seeing the fuse, standing too close to the fire.

The only place we could go was back to my grandma's, but my mom said she needed time to figure things out. Something inside me tightened the moment she said it.

There was a strange heaviness between my mom and her stepfather, tight and unresolved, like words that had never been spoken but never disappeared. I didn't know the whole story, but my body recognized the tension. My mom shared pieces. I didn't want to hear them, but I had already seen enough.

When I was ten or eleven, she told me she'd had to leave Grandma's house because it wasn't safe. She said she'd run from my step-grandpa when I was a baby, long before I could remember. There had been a moment when fear became immediate, undeniable. She'd lived in a small wooden shed on Grandma's land then, where I had also stayed as a baby. Just thinking about it made my chest tighten, my hands curl into fists.

That place held pieces of safety and pieces of fear.

When I got older, I never went inside that shed. It became storage over time, boxes stacked, broken things abandoned. Knowing what had once lived there made it impossible to see it as anything else.

Before long, the yelling started, sharp and loud. I watched

my step-grandpa shove my mom out the front door. I froze, then ran into my grandma's bathroom and shut the door.

I heard my mom shouting, "Let me talk to my daughter!"

When she came inside, her mascara streaked down her face. Her eyes were wide and glassy, her breath uneven, like she'd run through a storm. Her voice cracked in ways that made my stomach knot.

She looked straight at me.

"Are you coming with me?"

My thoughts scattered. Where would we go? I had school. Stephanie lived nearby. I just wanted something to stay the same.

"I want to stay."

I saw something in her break.

Something inside me fractured, too.

She turned and walked away.

I never meant to hurt my mom. I loved her, but I was clinging to the smallest sense of normal.

I carried the weight of that choice for years.

I talked to Lisa, but not much. I hadn't heard from my mom. I didn't know where she was, whether she was okay, or if she was ever coming back.

So I did what I knew how to do. I got up each morning. Got dressed. Went to school. Came home. Changed into loose clothes. Helped around the house. Followed the rules.

And that was fine.

But I felt hollow. Not angry. Not sad. Just numb. My body kept moving, but my heart stopped reaching.

When I finally opened up to Lisa, she recognized the weight I was carrying, even when I couldn't name it. Mostly, I talked about my mom. I told her I felt lost, scared, and alone. I'd been taught not to speak about what happened in my grandma's house. Not to name people or places. Not to tell the truth out loud.

Once, my older uncle gave me a black eye. He was angry about something, grabbed a red velvet ottoman from Grandma's bedroom, and swung it at me. It hit my face hard. My eye swelled as I pressed my hand to it, wishing the pain would disappear.

I was told to say I'd hit a doorknob.

So I learned to keep everything vague, sharing only feelings, never names, never details.

Lisa never pushed.

She understood more than I told her.

And that mattered.

She loved me like I was her own. Sometimes she took me to Mazzio's for lunch or dinner, and those moments felt ordinary in the best way, like I had a place in the world.

For my eighth-grade dance, she bought me a red dress and took me to get my hair done. I didn't know how to thank her. Gratitude felt unfamiliar. But I felt seen.

The dance floor was set up like a runway, two lines with an open space between them. When it was my turn, I danced without thinking. I smiled in a way I hadn't in a long time.

I saw Lisa, camera lifted, ready to capture the moment.

And I was happy.

For that night, at least, I was exactly where I needed to be. With Lisa's smile behind the lens and laughter filling the room, hope felt possible.

Life wasn't fixed. The struggles hadn't ended.

But I wasn't alone.

And for now, that was enough. One step at a time, I just kept going.

# THE SUNDAY I'LL NEVER FORGET

There was a shift that year. My step-grandpa's drinking had gotten worse, slipping past quiet tolerance and old excuses. Most of the time, my grandma knew. Sometimes, he hid it well. Other times, he didn't call. That silence was its own warning.

When he drank, the house stopped being safe. He became loud. Cruel. Violent.

I had learned to keep my distance, and as I got older, I had more choices. I started staying away on weekends, sleeping at friends' houses, keeping myself out of his reach.

He hated that.

He wanted me home. Cleaning. Visible. Useful.

I never imagined that one weekend away would cost me so much.

Then came the Sunday.

I will never forget the day that changed the trajectory of my life.

I came home like I always did. The walk back felt normal.

Quiet. But the second I stepped through the door, my body knew. The air was too still. The silence felt dangerous.

He was sitting in his chair, the television on but unwatched. A beer in his hand. Another on the table. His eyes met mine. Cold. Waiting.

He asked where I had been.

My answers were always careful. Short. Respectful. Measured.

But he was already angry. Not just drunk-angry, but wounded. Entitled. Explosive.

I had betrayed him by choosing to be away.

He stood up. His voice was loud, his words slurred.

I backed away. I knew that tone. I knew what came next.

He moved toward me, and I walked toward the back room, trying to stay calm. Trying to disappear. He followed, his voice rising with every step. He cornered me against the window, his face inches from mine.

His spit hit my cheek as he yelled.

"You don't need to be running around all weekend. You belong here. This is your home. You should be cleaning. Helping. Not acting like you're grown."

"I asked Grandma. I got permission."

In his eyes, I had crossed a line. Independence looked like rebellion to him. Freedom looked like disrespect.

I had asked for one night away, then begged for a second. I was just trying to breathe. I knew my grandma must have paid for giving me permission. That knowing still hurts.

"You're nothing but a slave in this house," he said.

Slave.

That word hit harder than his fist ever could. I wasn't just being yelled at. I was being erased. Reduced. Degraded.

I felt the blood drain from my face. A ringing filled my ears.

I didn't cry. I stood there, silent, while he turned and walked away like it was nothing.

But it wasn't nothing.

Something inside me shifted. Not pain. Knowing.

And knowing is stronger.

I knew this wasn't love. This wasn't home. This would not be my forever.

My grandma came in and tried to stand up for me. "Leave her alone!" she shouted. He pushed her, and she managed to get him into the living room. My heart raced, and I followed.

My uncles sat frozen on the couch.

In full rage, my step-grandpa grabbed a broom and began swinging it, hitting everyone. Then it dropped sideways onto the couch. He slammed his foot down on it, trying to break it. His leg buckled. That only made him angrier.

My grandma managed to get him outside, but he was yelling and slapping her.

When he came back in, I was in the kitchen. He was still raging. Coming straight at me. My grandma was still outside. That terrified me.

I lifted my hands, trying to protect myself.

His hands were around my neck.

I don't know how long it lasted. Seconds. Maybe longer. I couldn't breathe. Everything blurred.

Then, police officers stormed in and told him to step away and put his hands up. He didn't listen. He kept fighting. It took several officers to force him to the ground, their voices sharp and urgent as they restrained and cuffed him.

When they put him into the back of the patrol car, officers came inside to speak with us. My grandma turned to me and said, "It's okay. You can tell them."

We stepped onto the porch. The porch he had built with his own hands. I sat on the wooden steps.

I told them he had been touching me in ways no child should ever be touched.

After I said it out loud, everything went quiet.

No one rushed me. No one touched me.

I remember the sound of pens moving. The heaviness of the air. The way my hands would not stop shaking.

Something had been spoken that could never be taken back.

# PERMISSION TO SPEAK

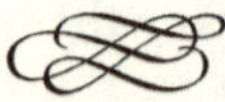

They took him to jail, and the trailer fell still.

Not peaceful. Hollow.

The quiet felt unfamiliar, heavy in a way I didn't know how to name.

The next day, and the day after that, my uncles and I didn't go to school. We stayed home while my grandma rested. We played video games, sitting close together on the floor. She looked exhausted in a way I hadn't seen before. Not just tired, but worn down by too many years of surviving the same storms.

At school, counselors explained that detectives would speak with us individually.

My step-grandpa kept calling. He told my grandma he didn't understand why he was being held in that unit. Her voice changed when she spoke about him. Softer. Uncertain. She had told me to tell the truth, but now it felt like that permission had been quietly taken back.

The detective who interviewed me looked me straight in the eyes and said, "If you want a future, you need to get out."

I nodded. I didn't know how to respond.

He handed me his card. The weight of it surprised me. I held onto it longer than I needed to. That small rectangle of paper felt like the first lifeline I'd ever been given.

I could see the change in my grandma. The woman who had protected me for so long felt farther away now. Her loyalty pulled her in two directions. Years of fear, silence, and compromise sat heavily on her shoulders. I didn't blame her. Family is complicated. Love is complicated.

Still, something inside me was shifting.

Each time detectives returned, I was led into a small room. Cold. Windowless. Fluorescent lights buzzing overhead. They spoke calmly, carefully. Their questions carried weight. They asked about moments I wished I could forget. About things that hurt too much to say out loud.

I answered as best I could. My heart raced. Sometimes my voice shook. Sometimes I wanted to disappear back into silence. But I stayed. Because I knew it mattered.

After those interviews, I didn't feel lighter.

I felt more alone.

My mom was still gone. My grandma felt distant. My step-grandpa was behind bars. Nothing felt resolved. Nothing felt safe. The truth had been spoken, but the cost of it was settling in.

I learned then how much courage it takes to speak when no one wants to hear. How telling the truth can fracture what little stability remains.

Permission to speak wasn't about the police or the counselors.

It wasn't about rules or investigations.

It was about giving myself the right to be heard.

To trust my own voice.

To be believed.

To stop carrying the weight alone.
And to begin something that felt impossible at the time.
Healing.

# NOWHERE TO GO BUT FORWARD

On the last day of ninth grade, I ran away.

There was no dramatic exit. No one chased me. No one knew I wasn't coming back.

I just left.

I walked out of school with the clothes on my back and whatever I'd shoved into my backpack. I didn't look back. Not because I didn't care, but because looking back would have broken me. My grandma had chosen to let my step-grandpa return, and the detective's words stayed with me.

I had to get out.

That summer, I floated. I stayed with friends when I could. Couches. Spare rooms. Anywhere I was welcome. I learned how to take up as little space as possible. I smiled when it was expected, stayed quiet when it mattered, and never asked for more than people were willing to give.

Still, I carried everything I'd left behind.

As summer stretched on, the safety of temporary places began to thin. People's patience has a shelf life. My name was still tied to a school, a past, a place I could not return to. And I had no idea where my mom was.

I started asking around. Quietly at first, then with urgency. I called numbers I wasn't sure still worked. I reached out to people I hadn't spoken to in months. I followed every rumor, every possible lead.

I needed her.

Not just because school was starting. But because even after everything, some part of me still hoped she might choose me. I imagined a version of her who would pull me close and say, "I've got you now."

I didn't know if that version of her still existed.

And I didn't know how long I could keep waiting to find out.

I found her number scribbled in the back of a notebook I'd nearly thrown away. My hand hovered over the phone longer than I want to admit before I finally pressed call.

It rang once.

Then again.

Then again.

Each ring stretched thin, like it might snap. I held my breath, waiting for a voice I wasn't sure I'd ever hear again.

"Hello?"

"Mom? Irene?"

"Yes… who is this?"

"It's me. It's your daughter."

"Um… how are you?"

I didn't know what she'd been told, or if she'd been told anything at all. I couldn't explain what had happened at my grandma's. I didn't have the strength. So I asked the only thing that mattered.

"Can I come live with you?"

The silence on the other end felt longer than the ringing had. I could hear her breathing, faint and unsure.

My stomach tightened.

She didn't say no.

She said, "Let me talk to him."

That *him* was the boyfriend she was living with. He had two sons who stayed there sometimes. I didn't know them. They didn't know me. But I wasn't looking for comfort. I was looking for somewhere to land.

She lived in a house near a main road, where traffic never stopped. It wasn't a trailer or an apartment. It was a house. That alone made it feel like a different kind of possibility.

The front door creaked when it opened. Wooden crosses hung above every doorway, each entrance marked like a quiet warning or a prayer. I learned quickly not to ask questions.

There wasn't a room for me. His sons and I shared. That was enough. I had learned not to expect space that belonged only to me.

I was about to start tenth grade. A new school. Another beginning. I told myself this would be different.

My mom worked long hours as a waitress. Her boyfriend's sons came every other week. He didn't ask much about me. I didn't ask much about him.

I tried to blend in. To stay useful. To stay unnoticed.

And for a little while, I let myself believe this might last.

By the time I found my mom again, I already knew how to live out of a backpack. I didn't yet know how often I would need that skill.

# MAYBE THIS TIME

My mom still drank. She still smoked. The smell of stale cigarettes clung to the furniture, the walls, even to her hair when she hugged me, mixed with the amber vanilla of her body spray. I didn't expect her to change. I had learned to accept what was offered and be grateful for it.

Her boyfriend made homemade tortillas, hot and soft, slightly burnt at the edges, and rolled them into bean burritos. I liked them more than I ever said out loud. Small things like that softened the days, made life feel more manageable.

For a while, life felt settled.

Stephanie, my safe person, visited. I met new friends at school. We went out, laughed, and stayed up too late. I was learning how to exist in a place that didn't already know my story. The town had an energy I couldn't name, but I felt it. It felt open. Fresh. Like something might be possible.

Best of all, no one there knew who I had been.

They didn't know about the trailer. Or the bruises. Or the police. Or the detective who pressed a card into my hand and told me I wouldn't have a future if I stayed. I didn't have to carry any of that in their eyes.

I had friends. People wanted me around. For the first time in a long time, my days weren't about survival. They were about being present.

Maybe I was starting to live.

Maybe I could be a girl with a future.

Still, something lingered.

On nights when the house was too quiet, or when the memories came without warning, the weight returned. My mom's drinking didn't help. Sometimes she became someone I barely recognized, her voice sharper, her patience thin.

I stayed out of the way. I focused on school. I held tightly to the ordinary moments. Stephanie kept me grounded. She reminded me that I was more than where I came from. Still, when I looked in the mirror, I saw a girl who had learned too much too early. A girl still searching for where she belonged.

Maybe this time would be different.

Maybe I didn't have to know how it would work yet.

One day, after we'd been hanging out, my friends were dropping me off. As we pulled up, one of them hesitated.

"Sorry," they said. "Can I drop you off at Pep Boys instead?"

"Um... yeah? Why?"

They shifted in their seat. "You don't know? People say your house is connected to some things."

"What things?"

They shook their head. "You don't want to know."

I didn't ask anything else. I wasn't sure I believed it, and I wasn't about to bring it up to my mom. I knew her boyfriend rode a motorcycle. I knew he worked, though I didn't know where or what. I knew enough to understand that questions didn't always come with answers.

So I kept it to myself.

It became another quiet weight, something I wasn't ready to examine too closely. I wasn't trying to be naive. I was trying to stay afloat.

Sometimes, when I was alone, I wondered what else lived just beyond what I could see. What else didn't I know?

But for now, I held onto what I could. The smell of warm tortillas. Stephanie's laughter. New friends who only knew the girl I was becoming.

Maybe this time, that would be enough.

# SHADOWS IN THE NIGHT

My mom and her boyfriend fought a lot. Most nights, their voices carried through the walls, sometimes spilling straight into my room. It was a school night, and all I wanted was sleep, but rest was hard to come by.

I don't know if my mom was scared or if something deeper made the fights so loud and raw. Eventually, either the noise stopped, or I fell asleep while they were still yelling.

I learned how to make myself small. How to disappear into the quiet corners of the room. I didn't want to be part of it. I didn't want to witness the breaking of the people who were supposed to protect me.

I pushed my feelings down until they dulled. I wanted things to feel normal, and this fractured, unstable version of life slowly became my definition of it.

Some days were manageable. Others were overwhelming. When it became too much, I stayed with friends or kept myself busy, anything to avoid the tension waiting at home.

Asking my mom for money was hard. She did what she could, but there was never enough. I didn't understand the strain between her and her boyfriend, but I knew it weighed on everything.

I asked for clothes sometimes. Nothing special. Just enough to blend in. At school, some girls showed up polished and put together. I just wanted to look like I belonged. Friends passed things along when they could, and my mom helped when she was able.

I held on to those small kindnesses. Borrowed clothes. Laughter between classes. Moments that felt lighter. I was learning how to endure without falling apart, telling myself that things might eventually change. But deep down, I knew drifting like this couldn't last forever.

I grew close to a girl at school. Someone I trusted. Someone who made the days feel easier. I shared small pieces of my story with her, nothing whole, just fragments. Even that felt like relief.

I don't know if her mom overheard or if my friend told her because she thought it might help. But when I was called into the school counselor's office, I understood that this was bigger than me keeping secrets.

The counselor looked at me kindly and asked how I was doing. I wanted to tell the truth. I was terrified of what would happen if I did.

That moment marked a shift. I wasn't the only one carrying it anymore. And once something is seen, it can't be unseen.

I had been taught to stay quiet. Don't tell. Silence meant safety. Then I thought about Lisa. How she had noticed me. How she had cared. She wasn't there anymore, but I wondered if this counselor could be someone like her.

Fear answered first.

I stayed quiet. I told her I was fine. Thank you for checking.

I wasn't fine.

Every question felt like pressure. Every gentle pause made

my chest tighten. I wanted to say everything, to finally let it spill out, but fear kept my voice locked away. What if telling made things worse? What if no one believed me?

So I stayed silent. Smiled when expected. Nodded when asked.

Quiet. Invisible. Protected, or so I told myself.

Still, somewhere beneath it all, a small spark remained. The thought that maybe one day, I wouldn't have to hide anymore.

# QUIET BETWEEN THE LINES

The counselor's office felt cold but safe, a strange contrast to the storm I carried inside. She asked questions I wasn't sure I was ready to answer, so I chose my words carefully. Measured. Guarded. I said only what I could manage.

I wasn't ready to tell everything. Not yet.

She paid attention in a way that made me uneasy, not because it felt wrong, but because it felt unfamiliar. When I finished speaking, the silence that followed was heavy. I didn't know what it meant or what would come next.

I walked out holding a small hope, tucked into the spaces of what I had not said.

Nothing changed right away. I still moved through the halls. Still answered questions with nods or a practiced "I'm fine." But something had shifted, subtle and internal, like a thread loosening where everything had once been tightly knotted.

I wanted to believe I could begin untangling the silence I had lived inside for so long. That I could let someone see more than the surface. But fear stayed close. Fear of being judged. Fear of not being believed.

At night, I lay awake staring at the ceiling, imagining what it might feel like to say everything out loud. To set the weight down. To be heard without someone turning away.

So I stayed quiet. Not because I wanted to, but because quiet still felt safer than truth.

My mom and I both loved Mexican food. One night, we went to Chelino's for dinner. The warm lights, the smell of spices, and the sound of laughter around us created a small pocket of ease. I let myself settle into it. The salsa. The crunch of chips. The way my mom smiled across the table.

For a little while, the past loosened its grip.

I could feel how much I had changed. How aware I'd become of every movement, every reaction. I moved through life carefully, like someone balancing on a narrow line. I wasn't a perfect child. I had grown up largely on my own, learning from adults who drifted in and out, absorbing lessons I hadn't asked for.

Life was messy. Broken in places. And still, in small moments, it could feel whole.

My mom and I were still learning about each other. Two people trying to find their way through a fog. There were things we never said because they were too heavy to hold in daylight. Most days, we pressed them down and moved on.

But when she drank, the restraint disappeared. Anger surfaced fast and loud. I tried to soften it. Tried to say the right thing. Nothing worked.

I didn't know how to fix it. I didn't know if anyone could.

There were rare moments when the anger loosened. Brief, fragile openings. One night, we stayed up late in the kitchen after the house had gone quiet. The air felt still. For once, it wasn't about tension or disappointment.

She talked about her younger years. About who she was

before everything hardened. I listened. Fully. And in that moment, I saw her not just as my mother, but as someone shaped by her own losses.

It didn't repair anything. It didn't erase what had already happened. But it softened something inside me.

She told me about her father and the trees. The way moss hung low. The way branches moved like they were whispering. Maybe that was where my love of trees began. Not just because they were rooted, but because they held their stories quietly, asking you to be still long enough to notice.

Her voice changed when she spoke about them. Softer. Her eyes didn't pass over me. They stayed present, somewhere remembered.

I'd only met my biological grandfather twice. I didn't know what kept him distant or which stories never reached me. But listening to her that night, I felt connected to something unnamed. As if even in broken histories, roots could still exist.

My grandma's place wasn't always peaceful, but the garden was. I remembered digging into the soil, pulling weeds, and watering rows of vegetables. Checking on cows and chickens before dinner. I loved that part of my life. The animals. The care. The responsibility.

Tending to things taught me something. That care mattered. That steadiness mattered. That gentleness could exist even when the world felt sharp.

I didn't know then that I was learning how to stay.

I carried that knowledge forward, even when everything else felt uncertain.

# ROOTS AND RECKONINGS

The morning after the fight, I went back to the house to get my things for school.

I had left the night before without shoes. Without a bra. Without my notebook or my backpack. I did not think. I just left.

I told myself I would be quick. Grab what I needed and go. I did not know what had happened after I left. I did not know if my mom was okay. I had not heard from her.

I wondered if she was hurt. I wondered if she was awake. I wondered if she was alone. I wondered if she had called my name after I walked out.

A friend drove me. The car was quiet. I stared out the window and tried not to imagine what I had not seen.

My hands were cold, even though it wasn't cold outside.

When we turned onto the street, I knew something was wrong.

Police cars lined the curb in front of the house. Not rushing. Red and blue flashing lights. Just there. Parked at angles that blocked the driveway. Doors open. Officers standing still, alert.

My chest tightened as I stepped out of the car. It felt like walking toward something that had already made up its mind about me.

"What's going on?" I asked.

An officer turned toward me. His voice was firm but calm.

"Ma'am, stop right there. Do you live here?"

"Yes," I said. "My mom lives here. I live here."

He studied my face for a moment. Then he said, "Your mom is in the hospital."

The words did not make sense at first. They floated in the air like they belonged to someone else.

"What?" I said. "Why?"

"There was an incident last night," he said. "Were you here?"

I nodded slowly. "Yes. They were fighting. I left."

"She's stable," he said. "Her arm is broken."

The air left my lungs. Broken. The word echoed longer than it should have.

"And him?" I asked. I did not say his name.

"He's still inside. When he comes out, he'll be arrested."

I looked at the front door. Everything I owned was inside. My clothes. My notebook. My shoes. The pieces of normal I was still trying to hold together.

"I just need my things for school," I said quietly.

"I'm sorry," he said. "You can't go inside right now."

That was when I understood. Not fully. Not in words. But in my body.

I was not going back in.

My friend touched my arm. "Come on," she said. "We'll figure it out."

We went back to her house. I borrowed what I could. A hoodie. Shoes. A sports bra. Enough to get through the day.

Clothes that fit, but didn't belong to me.

Then we drove to school.

I sat in class pretending nothing had happened. I wrote notes. I answered questions. I kept my head down. No one asked why my shoes were different. I was grateful for that.

By the end of the day, I knew something had shifted.

The place I had left was no longer a place I could return to.

And the version of me who walked out the night before wasn't coming back either.

# WHEN THE WALLS CLOSED IN

I walked into school like everything was normal. Like I hadn't just stood outside my house surrounded by police cars. Like I hadn't been told, my mom was in the hospital with a broken arm. Like I wasn't wearing the same clothes from the night before. I walked in like I'd done my homework and slept through the night.

My friend handed me a notebook and a hoodie.

"You good?"

I nodded. That was enough for both of us.

I made it through first period. And second. I don't remember

a single thing the teachers said. My head felt foggy, like I was watching the day from somewhere far away.

I was called to the office.

Two women were sitting there. One of them smiled and gently introduced herself as someone from Child Protective Services. My stomach dropped. Not here. Not now.

She asked if we could talk somewhere private.

My world shifted again. Quietly this time. Not with screams

or sirens, but with soft voices and manila folders that felt heavier than anything I'd carried.

The woman's voice was calm, but her words still landed hard. She said my mom had come to the school from the hospital. She was injured. She was unstable. I hadn't shared anything, but apparently she had. And now they knew more than I was ready to say.

They told me there had been other reports. From people who knew what was happening in that house. People who had noticed things I thought I was hiding.

I didn't speak. I couldn't. I just stared.

Then she said it. Emergency protective custody.

It didn't feel real. I was just at school. My math homework

was due. I had lunch plans. My locker still held books I hadn't taken home. But none of that mattered anymore. I wouldn't be going back to class. I wouldn't be going home. I wouldn't be saying goodbye to my friends. Not even my mom.

Just like that, I was gone.

The women took me away without warning. Without time to grab anything. All I had were the clothes I was wearing and whatever strength I could find in that moment.

First, there were the metal detectors. I had to walk through one like I was in trouble, even though I hadn't done anything wrong. The buzzing and the hollow feeling in my stomach felt like punishment, even if they didn't call it that.

Then we took the elevator down. Down into something I didn't understand yet.

The doors opened onto a large, cold space that echoed. Other kids were there. Older. Younger. Loud. Quiet. All of us carrying something heavy.

One of the women explained everything quickly, as if it were just another day. My backpack was taken and stored. They showed me where I could pick out clothes that fit. Where I would shower. Where I would eat. Where I would sleep, a small room with beds lined up against the walls.

I didn't have my own space, but I wasn't expecting that.

A schedule was taped to the wall. Lights on. Lights off. Breakfast. School. Showers. Bed. Everything had a time. No choices. Just rules.

I was in the system now.

My first night, I didn't eat dinner. I didn't speak. The lump in my throat wouldn't go away. I knew if I opened my mouth, everything inside would spill out.

The room was full of quiet movement. Kids finding their spots. Some whispering. Some crying softly. I lay on my bed, staring at the ceiling, wondering how I got here. How I had stepped into a life that didn't feel like mine.

The staff was kind. Gentle voices. Calm instructions. I could tell they were trying. But kindness doesn't undo trauma. And being labeled safe doesn't mean you feel okay inside it.

Survival teaches you things. It wires you. We learn to build invisible walls made of silence, toughness, and instinct. We protect ourselves in ways no placement can replace.

We were young, but not fragile. We had seen too much. In the quiet corners of the night, where I was supposed to feel protected, I felt the weight of everything I had never said.

This wasn't safety. It was just another way of surviving.

I woke up to bright fluorescent lights and the sound of doors unlocking. Yes, the doors were locked at night.

We were told to make our beds, get dressed, and head to breakfast. I still didn't want to talk to anyone. When someone offered, I quietly said, "Thank you," or "No, thank you." Nothing more.

We were given clean clothes to change into before showers, then told to wait in a common sitting area until our turn was called.

Shower time came next. We waited in a sitting area surrounded by older kids. Girls and boys. Some laughing. Some dancing. I watched them move like the weight hadn't found them yet. I learned the "B walk" there, of all places.

Every day was the same. Wake up. Eat. Shower. Worksheets for school. No real classes. Just packets spread across a round table.

After a few weeks, I was assigned a case manager named Ferona. She was older but colorful. Bright clothes. Quirky glasses. Big earrings. Slip-on heels. She explained I needed a plan A and a plan B for placement, meaning where I would live next.

Plan A: family placement. Unfortunately, that wasn't possible for me. Plan B: a friend's mom. A single mom who said she'd take me in. The friend was only a little older than I was.

Ferona asked me to be patient. All the paperwork, home studies, and approvals took time. She promised she was working day and night to get me out of there as soon as possible.

But things were getting harder.

Some girls didn't like me. If I even glanced in the wrong direction, they looked for a fight. I learned quickly how to disappear. Sometimes I forgot where I was. Reality always snapped me back.

During showers, a guard stood outside the door. I guess it was for protection. I never understood why. I still don't.

Days blurred together, each one a mix of numb routine and quiet desperation. I kept my head down. Blended in. The laughter from the older kids sounded like freedom and trouble wrapped together.

Sometimes, when I was alone, the weight of everything crashed over me. I thought about my mom. About the fights.

About how I ended up here. I missed my old life, even the painful parts, because at least they were familiar.

I held onto whatever pieces of normal I could. I focused on schoolwork, even if it was just worksheets, because it gave me something to do. A distraction. I imagined a future where I wasn't stuck in this place. Where I had choices. Where I was safe.

Ferona was one of the few people who made me feel like someone was fighting for me. She listened without judgment and explained the process as clearly as she could. Still, the waiting was the hardest part. It made every day feel heavier.

Some nights, when the noise from the other girls grew too loud, or footsteps echoed down the hall, I stared at the ceiling and whispered, This isn't forever.

I clung to that hope, even when everything around me said otherwise.

I watched the other kids. My heart ached for them. So many stories carried in tired eyes. But I didn't let myself get close. Trust felt like a luxury I could no longer afford.

The days passed, and Christmas was coming. For the first time in a long while, there was a flicker of something new. A chance to leave this place and move into a foster home. It wasn't perfect, but it was a step toward something different.

A step toward hope.

I didn't know what lay ahead.

But I was ready to try.

# COUNTING DAYS

The fluorescent lights flickered on, the doors unlocked, and I moved through the same motions as every day before. I wondered if this was what my mom had felt like when she was in jail.

She had been arrested before because of her drinking. It wasn't a single mistake. Even then, I understood enough to know it mattered.

I was sitting at a round table, the chatter around me dull and distant, when I felt a tap on my shoulder. I looked up to see Ferona, my case manager.

"You're going to be placed today," she said softly.

I stared at her. Placed. "What does that mean?"

"Let's get your things," she said.

"Things?" I whispered. "Wait. I have things?"

She smiled gently. "They've been keeping your belongings safe. Come on."

We walked down the hallway together, our footsteps echoing off the walls. My chest felt heavy with uncertainty, but underneath it was something lighter. Hope, maybe. Or the beginning of it.

Ferona handed me a small box. Inside were a few belongings. My friend's hoodie. My backpack. A notebook I barely remembered bringing. It was strange seeing pieces of my life gathered like this, as if time had paused and waited.

The foster home was a long drive away. When we arrived, I stepped out with my backpack over my shoulder. The house was older, red brick, with a simple cement porch. It wasn't fancy, but it felt solid.

I would be staying with Laura, a friend from school, and sharing a room with her. Her mom, Tisha, was short and wore black, pointy-edged glasses that made her look sharper than she was. Her warm smile softened the unfamiliar space immediately.

In the living room were two couches, a coffee table, and a softly glowing Christmas tree in the corner. The house smelled like pine and cinnamon. For a moment, I forgot how I had arrived there.

"This is your new home," Ferona said quietly. "Take all the time you need."

I wasn't the same girl Laura had known. I didn't know how to act. I felt awkward and exposed, unsure of where to place myself. Still, I kept moving forward, because that was what I knew how to do.

They asked me to sit down.

"Are you hungry? We're ordering pizza tonight. Do you like pizza?"

Choices. Real ones.

"Yes," I said quickly.

"What kind would you like?"

I hesitated. "Whatever you're ordering is fine. Thank you for letting me stay."

Tisha looked at me through her funky glasses and smiled. "We're so happy you're here. We've been waiting a long time for you."

I didn't know what to say, but it felt good to be wanted.

That night, the sound of pizza boxes opening and the laughter around the table felt unfamiliar. I watched Laura joke with her brother, their family moving easily around one another. It looked like something I'd only seen from the outside before.

I wanted to feel at home, but home had never been simple for me.

As I ate my pizza and watched the glow of the Christmas lights reflect on their faces, I let myself hope, carefully.

I didn't know how long I would stay. Whether this was healing or just another pause. But I allowed myself to believe I belonged somewhere, even if only for now.

Ferona told Tisha that I would receive a clothing voucher. I didn't have much. Just what I wore and what fit in my backpack. I never returned to my mom's house. That door closed without ceremony.

Laura took me shopping. Sitting in a car, doing something normal, felt like a gift. I was given a small amount from the state to buy essentials. It wasn't much, but it was something. Jeans. Shirts. Socks. Basics. It felt like starting over with permission.

The state helped with Christmas, too. I know people meant well. But that holiday passed in a blur. I remember the tree and a few wrapped gifts with my name on them. I was grateful, but still suspended between surviving and settling.

I understood the system. I wasn't a little kid anymore. I wasn't easy. Older kids carry stories people hesitate to take on.

Ferona had explained it honestly. Plan A was family. When that door closed, plan B meant someone willing to step in.

Without either, I would have gone to a group home. Some kids wait there until they age out. That could have been me.

Foster parents receive support to help care for kids like me. It makes sense. But I still wondered if I was there because I was wanted, or because I was possible.

I landed in a good place. Ferona stayed consistent. Tisha was warm. Laura treated me the same as always. Over time, the house stopped feeling borrowed.

Eventually, I returned to school.

Laura walked beside me through the doors. She stayed close without saying much. The halls looked the same. I didn't.

No one stared. My friends saved me a seat at lunch and checked in without pressing. I noticed, even if I didn't know how to thank them. Still, an invisible distance followed me. Trauma has weight.

I met regularly with the school counselor. At first, I dreaded it. I didn't know how to explain myself. But she didn't rush me. She let silence exist.

I wasn't used to steady support. Or gentle care. Little by little, I felt less unarmored.

Life began to feel almost normal. Laura and I spent time with friends. Games. Late nights. Laughing too loud. Stephanie came around again, and it felt good to reconnect pieces of my past with this strange present.

Laura was older, so I moved with an older crowd. It made me feel grown, but it also pulled me into things I wasn't ready for. My grades hovered. Not failing. Not thriving. Existing.

At home, things felt steady at first. Tisha was kind. Her boyfriend was quiet. Alcohol had always been part of my world, so when it appeared again, it didn't surprise me.

By then, I was drinking too. Parties. Fitting in. Trying to feel free.

But the house began to feel smaller. Arguments surfaced

when alcohol was involved. Nothing violent, but enough to wake something familiar in my body. Tight chest. Shallow breathing. I recognized the warning signs even when I tried to dismiss them.

There wasn't always enough food. I didn't say anything. I knew how to manage. Still, the exhaustion added up. I wasn't sleeping much. Eventually, doctors gave me something to help.

One night, after drinking, I shared too much with one of Laura's friends. I explained that we weren't sisters by blood. That I was in foster care. I let pieces of my story slip.

When your life is fragile, honesty can be expensive.

Stephanie and I went camping at Sulphur for a few days. One of our old places. The quiet helped. It reminded me who I was before everything shifted.

When I came back, the house looked different.

My belongings were stuffed into a black trash bag on the front porch.

No explanation. No conversation. No warning.

Just my life, packed up and waiting.

I didn't know it yet, but I was about to learn how fast temporary can disappear.

# BLACK TRASH BAG AND SILENT GOODBYES

That was it.

Everything I had, my clothes, my toothbrush, the comfort hoodie I wore too often, the small things that had just started to feel like mine, was stuffed into a black trash bag and left on the porch, like I was something meant to be discarded. No message. No goodbye. Just done.

Stephanie's face went still.

"Seriously?" she said under her breath.

Her mom parked the car but left the engine running. We sat there for a moment, staring at the lump of plastic as if it might explain itself.

It didn't.

I got out slowly and picked it up. It was heavy, not just with belongings, but with something else too. It felt heavier than it should have. Heavier than clothes. Heavier than fabric and toothpaste and borrowed hope.

I didn't call Ferona.

I didn't have the energy to explain. Or defend myself. Or make sense of something that already felt decided.

I asked to use Stephanie's phone and called Mia.

Mia, my close friend from school, lived with her sister and had always been someone I could count on.

"Mia… can I come stay with you?"

There was a pause on the other end.

"Yeah," she said carefully. "Is everything okay?"

"No," I whispered. "I'll explain when I get there."

Stephanie didn't ask questions. Her mom popped the trunk so I could set the bag inside, then waited while I climbed back into the car. The drive was quiet, but not uncomfortable. It was the kind of silence that carries understanding without asking for details.

I think Stephanie's mom understood this kind of pain. Maybe not the specifics, but the feeling of being pushed out without warning.

Mia was waiting outside when we pulled up. She opened the door and stepped forward, concern written all over her face. Her sister stood behind her, arms crossed, eyes steady. No hesitation.

"Get in here," her sister said. "You're safe."

I stepped inside, the bag still in my hand, and for the first time since seeing it on the porch, my breathing slowed.

I didn't know if CPS knew I wasn't there anymore. I didn't know if Tisha had called to say I wasn't wanted. I didn't ask.

I didn't want to know.

I didn't want to go back to the group home. The locked doors. The fluorescent lights. The scheduled showers. The quiet that pressed in and never let up.

I didn't want to be a number again. A file. Another girl carrying her life in a trash bag.

That bag had followed me too many times. It was starting to feel like my name.

I didn't want to leave my school. I was doing well. I had friends. I was holding things together.

Part of me thought I could disappear for a while. Stay unnoticed. Be normal.

Eventually, I learned what happened.

The friend I'd opened up to that night had talked to Laura. I must have said too much. About the drinking. The fighting. The lack of food. About how Laura and I weren't sisters by blood, just friends before foster sisters.

I never meant to hurt anyone.

I never meant for my truth to cost me a place to land.

But Laura must have felt betrayed. Something private had been carried outside our home, and in the system, perception matters. She and her mom had opened their doors to me, and I brought scrutiny with me.

Maybe that's what made the trash bag appear on the porch. Maybe not. I'll never fully know.

What I do know is this: I told the truth, and I lost a home. That lesson stayed with me for a long time.

Now I was hiding. From the state. From Ferona. From whatever came next. I stayed at Mia's, kept my head down, and went to school as if nothing had changed.

But it had.

A few days later, there was a knock at the door.

# FOUND

The knock came like a warning. Not loud. Not rushed. Three soft taps that made my chest tighten. Beforc I even looked, I knew it was Ferona.

The guilt arrived before I reached the door. The shame. The fear. I wasn't ready to face her. I wasn't ready to explain anything. But she already knew. She always seemed to know more than I said out loud.

When I opened the door, there she was. Same colorful outfit. Same wild glasses. The same calm presence that made you feel like things might be okay, even when they weren't.

She didn't yell. She didn't look disappointed. She just looked at me.

"I'm not mad," she said. "But we need to talk."

I nodded, barely breathing. Mia stood quietly behind me. Her sister lingered in the hallway, unsure what this meant for all of us.

Ferona didn't scold. She didn't rush. She listened.

And for the first time in a while, I didn't feel like I was running. I didn't know what would happen next, but I had been found. Someone knew where I was. Someone was still looking out for me. Even if I didn't know how to accept it, I wasn't invisible anymore.

Ferona stepped just inside the door. I could tell by the way she shifted her weight that what she had to say wasn't going to land easily.

She cleared her throat gently. "Irene… I found a placement. It's a group home. Just one city over."

My stomach dropped.

Group home.

I knew what that meant. Locked doors. Echoing voices. Lights that hummed too bright. Rules for everything. The kind of place where you follow directions and wait to be moved again.

My body stiffened before I could stop it.

"How long?" I asked.

She hesitated. "It's temporary. While we process things. This home is different. It's on land. More open. It's not like the last one."

It didn't matter. Whatever fragile sense of normal I had been holding onto slipped away.

Sophie stepped forward, her voice firm but steady. "She can stay here. I'll take her. She doesn't have to leave."

Ferona softened, but her voice stayed even. "I wish it worked that way, Sophie. I really do. But it doesn't. There's paperwork. A home study. Background checks. It's a process."

"What if we start the process now?" Sophie pressed. "She's already here. She's safe."

Ferona looked between us, then lowered her gaze. "Is it just the two of you living here?"

"No," Sophie said. "My boyfriend lives here too."

That was it.

Ferona nodded slowly. "I'm sorry. For a youth like Irene to

live here, especially with her case file, you'd need to be married. That's part of the placement criteria. Her case is sensitive."

"Married?" Sophie repeated, stunned. "Why does that even matter?"

Ferona's voice dropped. "I can explain in more detail, but not in front of the girls."

I felt the walls closing in again. Not physically. Systemically. Like I was something too complicated. Too high-risk. Too much. All I wanted was to stay. But nothing was that simple for someone like me.

It was time to grab my black trash bag. Always the same bag. Like it defined my worth, reducing my life to what I could carry in one trip.

Ferona stood nearby, watching quietly. She didn't rush me. She never did. Her job was heavy. I could tell. I often wondered what brought her there. Had she been a child of the system? Had she lost someone? Witnessed something that made her want to help kids like me?

She carried the weight of a hundred stories. Maybe more. But she showed up.

Maybe she was doing good.

But good doesn't always feel gentle when you're the one being moved.

In that moment, I had no family, and that meant I couldn't run free. I was a ward of the state. They needed to know where I was, who I was with, and that I was safe.

I was safer than I had ever been. Safe from drinking. From chaos. From silence after the fights. From too much and not enough.

Safe. But not staying.

As I scrunched the bag closed, a memory surfaced, uninvited but sharp.

The courtroom.

One of the early hearings, back when this all began. I sat with my legs swinging under the bench while strangers walked in and out. Everyone had questions. Everyone had forms.

My mom didn't have a home. She did what she could. Stayed where she could. But in the eyes of the state, that wasn't enough.

At one court date, my mom and I stood on opposite sides with a judge between us. Her voice was serious. Final. That day, she signed her rights away.

Not because she didn't love me.

But because she couldn't keep me.

Because life had been cruel to her, too. A single mom with nowhere to go, carrying traumas the world never saw. She couldn't give the court what it needed to see. So she gave me to the state.

I remember her hands trembling when she signed. I remember searching her face, wondering if she would look up and change her mind.

She didn't.

She couldn't.

I think, in some way, that was her version of love. Letting go because she had to, not because she wanted to.

Or maybe that's the story I built so I could survive being left.

The car door closed behind me, snapping me back into the present.

Ferona put the car in drive, and we pulled away from the curb in silence, headed to another city, another home, another chapter.

# THE EDGES OF BELONGING

We pulled up to what looked like a regular house. Nothing official or sterile from the outside. No big signs. No city building markers. Just a house sitting quietly off the road, surrounded by a bit of land.

But once we stepped inside, it was clear this wasn't just a house. The interior had been turned into a facility for kids who had nowhere else to go. It was structured. Monitored. Organized. Built for supervision, not softness.

I didn't let myself hope. I had done that before.

Ferona stood beside me, clipboard in hand, her face tired but kind. I could tell this wasn't easy for her either. She gave me space instead of pushing me forward. Maybe she understood more than she let on. Or maybe she had simply seen too many girls arrive this way.

At that point, I had no family advocating for me. My mom didn't have a home. She stayed where she could, did what she could, and tried in her own way. But on paper, where decisions were made, that still wasn't enough.

The door clicked shut behind me with a weight I couldn't name.

They walked me through intake again. My backpack and black trash bag were taken and searched. They handed me a set of clothes. Nothing special, but clean. I was shown the girls' rooms, the shower area, and the schedule for meals and schooling.

Same structure. Same rules. Different address.

This place wasn't like the last one. It was smaller. Quieter. There were only a few of us, and most were babies or toddlers. Temporary placements while the state figured out what came next for them. Staff rotated in and out, feeding, soothing, watching the clock. At meals, some were held or fed in high-chairs. Others sat at the table with workers.

I sat alone. Old enough to follow the rules. Young enough to still be waiting.

We weren't grouped by age, but by circumstance.

There were no personal touches. No family pictures. No chipped mugs, someone loved too much to throw away. Just the essentials.

The other kids glanced at me when I walked through the common area. Some with curiosity. Some with nothing. Just another girl with a bag and a file.

I was the oldest one there.

The second oldest was three years old.

Three.

My roommate was a toddler with curls and wide, watchful eyes. She clutched a stuffed animal like it was the only steady thing in her world.

I don't know why that hit me so hard.

Maybe because I had been her once. Small. Wordless. Carried from place to place without understanding why.

Maybe because I was used to chaos, to loud voices and instability. But this was different. This was a baby who didn't even have the words yet for what had happened to her.

I chose a top bunk.

Unpacked slowly. A folded shirt that wasn't mine. A notebook I barely remembered bringing. Socks that didn't match.

None of it felt like a life.

But it was all I had.

At dinner, I sat at the edge of a long table. Quiet. Watching. Listening. I didn't speak much, and no one asked me to.

That night, lying in a bed that wasn't mine, staring at the ceiling, I wondered how long I'd be here. Weeks? Months?

Would anyone visit? Would anyone care? And if I disappeared, would anyone notice?

Days turned into nights. Wake up. Eat. Sit. Shower. Sleep. Repeat.

My anger grew.

At first, it wasn't loud. Just a dull ache behind my ribs.

Then it became hot.

Not screaming heat. Not breaking things heat.

The kind that sits in your throat. The kind that makes your jaw clench when no one is talking to you.

Questions circled that had no answers.

What's wrong with me? Why didn't anyone want to keep me? Why wasn't I enough for someone to fight for?

And underneath all of that was something harder to admit:

Why did everyone else get chosen, and I kept getting moved?

Sometimes, I caught my reflection in the mirror. I couldn't look for long. My eyes felt unfamiliar, like they belonged to someone older. Someone tired in a way that didn't match her age.

There was anger in them. And something else.

Resignation.

I turned away before the thoughts could finish forming.

I didn't feel like a person. I felt like paperwork. A placement. A case number.

And after a while, I started to believe that's all I was.

Then Ferona came.

Her voice was soft. Familiar in a place that wasn't. She sat across from me, clipboard on her lap, studying my face like she was trying to measure what hadn't broken yet.

"I just wanted to check on you," she said. "I don't have any news, but I'm working on it. I haven't stopped."

I nodded.

I wanted to ask her how long a person can be "temporary" before it becomes permanent.

I didn't.

I didn't know what to say. Thank you for remembering me. Thank you for coming to see the girl with the black trash bag and too many pages in her file.

Her presence mattered.

Even without answers. Even without promises.

It reminded me I was still a person. Not just paperwork.

She stayed a little longer.

We didn't say much.

But for a few minutes, I wasn't invisible.

# WHEN THE WALLS BREAK

The news didn't come the way I thought it would. There was no dramatic reveal. No smile on anyone's face.

I'd broken down in the hallway, my back pressed against the cold wall, my arms wrapped around my knees. The tears came fast. Too many held back. Too many days of pretending I was okay. I didn't even know why I was crying. Maybe it was everything. Maybe it was the weight finally asking to be felt.

A staff member saw me. She sat down nearby. Didn't say much. Just waited.

When I finally looked up, eyes swollen and burning, she said, "Ferona's here. She has news for you."

With Ferona, news was never small. It meant a placement. A move. A decision already made.

My chest tightened. I wasn't sure I wanted to hear it. But I stood anyway. I had learned to get up, even when I wanted to stay down.

I followed her down the hall, wiping my face with the sleeve of my sweatshirt. I could still feel the tightness in my throat. The way my body had folded in on itself. I hated crying in front of people. But something had cracked. And once the pieces fell, I couldn't gather them fast enough.

Ferona stood in the office, her usual clipboard clutched in one hand. She looked at me the way she always did, with that mix of purpose and softness. Like she had to be strong. Like she wished she could make it easier.

"There's a home," she said gently. "It's not too far. They have space. It's not permanent, but it's a step forward."

A step forward.

I nodded. I couldn't tell if what rose in my chest was relief or fear. It felt like both, braided together.

I didn't ask what they knew about me or what I was walking into. Part of me was too tired to brace for another answer.

"Can I pack now?"

"Yes," she said. "We'll leave this afternoon."

I walked back to my room. The room I shared with a toddler barely out of diapers. My three-year-old roommate was playing on the floor. She looked up and smiled, unaware that I would be gone before dinner. That I was always meant to be passing through.

She followed me everywhere when we were together, dragging her blanket behind her like a shadow. At night, she cried until I sat beside her bunk. Her small fingers wrapped around mine like I could keep the world steady. I stayed longer than I was supposed to. Sitting on the floor. Listening to her breathing even out.

She needed me.

And in her eyes, I wasn't temporary.

For a little while, she made me feel important.

I grabbed the black trash bag from the closet and gathered my few belongings. Clothes from the donation bin. A toothbrush. My notebook. I didn't have much, but I folded everything carefully anyway. As if the way I handled it could prove it mattered. As if I mattered.

Ferona and I drove in silence, the hum of the road filling the spaces between us. I didn't want to know too much. Knowing only made the leaving harder.

We pulled into a quiet neighborhood. Trimmed lawns. Wind chimes. Wide sidewalks. The house was beautiful. Red brick with white shutters. A flower bed blooming by the porch. A welcome mat that didn't look worn down by too many feet.

It didn't feel temporary.

It felt like someone lived there on purpose.

Renae opened the door. She was in her early sixties, with auburn hair and a soft, steady smile. She wasn't married. She lived alone. But something about her presence filled the space with warmth.

"Hi, Irene," she said. "I'm so glad you're here."

She didn't force a hug. She simply opened the door wider and stepped aside. Like she had been waiting.

Inside, everything was clean and cozy. She led me to a bedroom.

My bedroom.

A real bed with matching sheets. A blanket folded neatly at the end. A small desk in the corner. A window looking out onto the backyard where a bird feeder swayed gently in the breeze.

The pantry was full. Not just the basics. Snacks. Cereal with bright labels. Brand names I recognized. She told me I could help myself to anything.

Anything.

I learned she had taken all the required classes to foster. She wanted to be involved. She wanted to do this right. Her home was calm. Her heart seemed wide open.

She hosted family dinners. Siblings and cousins gathered

around the table, laughing. She told me that when I was ready, there would always be a seat for me.

It didn't erase everything I had been through.

But I didn't feel like a problem to solve.

I felt like a person being welcomed.

That night, I lay in bed thinking about my three-year-old roommate. Her tiny voice. The way she looked up at me like I was her safe place.

I wasn't.

But I tried to be.

Even in that warm room, in a house that smelled like fresh linen and soft perfume, I couldn't sleep. That's the part no one tells you about bouncing from place to place. Your body forgets how to rest, even when the threat is gone. Sleep feels dangerous. Like you might wake up somewhere new.

Again.

I rolled over and looked around. Everything matched. The rug. The curtains. The comforter. The framed pictures weren't crooked. The closet had empty hangers waiting to be used. There was food in the pantry. My own toothbrush in the bathroom. A door that shut fully without sticking.

It should have felt like home.

But I wasn't sure what home meant anymore.

Still, something about that room stirred a memory. A feeling I hadn't let myself touch in years.

I was four years old in that photo. My birthday. A cake in front of me. My mom beside me. The man I called my father, though he wasn't. Not really. But I didn't know that then.

I was smiling in that picture. Round cheeks. Wide eyes. Joy untouched.

That kind of light didn't follow me into the years that came next.

But in that quiet room, in a house where someone chose to

take classes just to care for a girl like me, I felt a flicker of that little girl again.

Not lost. Not erased. Just buried beneath years of surviving.

Maybe she wasn't entirely gone. Maybe she had been waiting for a place gentle enough to come back.

## NEW STEPS, OLD HALLS

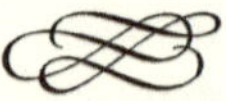

Returning to school felt strange. Not scary. Not exciting. Just strange. Like walking into a room I once knew, but with everything slightly out of place, including myself.

Renae's home had brought structure, safety, and peace. A warm meal. A quiet night. My own room. A door that locked from the inside, not the outside. And the best part? It was close enough that I could return to my old school. Peace didn't erase memory, but it made space for something new to begin.

Soon after I returned, the school counselor and principal called me in. They were kind, but I could see the concern in their eyes, the careful way they asked how I was doing. We all knew it wasn't just about school. It was about whether I would make it.

They offered me a plan so I could graduate early. After-school alternative classes. Credit recovery. A faster path out.

I heard what they didn't say: You've lost enough time. Let's not lose more.

I hadn't expected that. I wasn't sure I could pull it off. But I clung to it like something solid. Something that moved forward instead of sideways.

When I walked through the halls again, no one made a scene. I was no longer a mystery. Just the girl who left and came back. Again and again.

Familiar faces glanced at me differently now. Some with soft eyes. Maybe pity. Maybe curiosity. Maybe relief that it wasn't them. No one asked questions.

And I was grateful.

And I was angry.

Both can live in the same body.

Something was different this time. Not loud. Not dramatic. But steady.

I made a new friend who lived just a few streets over. Marie. She was easy to be around. She didn't ask where I'd been or what had happened. She just talked about normal things, what we were wearing to the game on Friday. Which song was stuck in our heads? Who was dating who?

She made life feel normal again.

And I didn't realize how hungry I was for normal until someone handed it to me without conditions.

Marie and I joined a competitive cheer squad together. Not through the school. An outside team. Something that belonged to us — not my file, not my case plan.

It felt good to move.

To shout.

To sweat.

To let my body do something besides brace for impact.

Practices were hard, but familiar. I'd done cheer before with Stephanie, and my muscles remembered. The stunts. The counts. The rhythm. The stretch of a solid tumble pass.

For two minutes on the mat, I wasn't a placement.

I was strong.

I was lifted.

I was caught.

At home, though, I kept thinking about the three-year-old back at the group home. Her tiny frame. The way she clutched her blanket. The way she followed me like I had answers.

I wondered if someone had chosen her yet.

Or if she was still waiting.

When I sat on the bed in the room Renae had given me, soft blankets tucked tight, a lamp with a dimmer switch glowing low — it sometimes felt like too much.

Too soft.

Too steady.

Too safe.

Sometimes she gently knocked on my door and asked if I wanted to watch TV. I usually said yes. Not because of the show, but because her presence felt consistent.

She didn't ask for explanations.

She didn't push.

She just sat.

We didn't talk much. We laughed sometimes. She had her routines. The way she loaded the dishwasher. The way she folded laundry into even stacks. The way she turned off the porch light every night before bed.

And as odd as it felt at first, I needed that.

I needed someone who woke up at the same time every morning. Someone who reminded me to eat. Someone who made sure the lights were off by ten.

It was foreign.

A steady adult who wasn't yelling.

Wasn't disappearing.

Wasn't bringing chaos through the door.

At first, I didn't trust it.

Peace feels suspicious when you've survived storms.

But it was healing.

And little by little, without ceremony, without announcements, without promises…

I let it in.

# LEARNING TO ASK

I began applying for jobs and eventually landed one at an Italian restaurant. It felt good to earn something of my own, to be out in the world in a new way. I saved up and bought a light purple Dodge Neon. It wasn't much, but it was mine. Well, almost. An estranged uncle who worked at a bank helped a little. He wasn't in my life in any meaningful way, but I reached out anyway.

I hated asking. But I was learning that independence sometimes begins with swallowing pride.

Soon, I was able to get my first cell phone. That should have been a moment of celebration. A phone meant freedom and connection. Exciting for a teen.

But for me, it meant something else.

It meant staring at a blank contact list. It meant typing my mom's name and not knowing what number to enter. It meant waiting for a call that never came.

I had no contact with her. Having a cell phone didn't change that. I thought if I had my own phone, maybe I could reach her.

Maybe she would call. But I was a ward of the state. Their responsibility. Their rules.

Even with a phone in my hand, I was still someone else's paperwork.

Ferona visited from time to time to make sure things were going okay. Sometimes the visits were quick. A few notes scribbled down. A nod. A smile. But sometimes, the topic turned to my mom.

And that was when something inside me snapped.

Once when she came, I couldn't even get myself out of the bathroom. I sat on the floor, back pressed against the tub, fists clenched, jaw tight.

I wasn't crying. I was shaking.

My heart pounded so hard it hurt. I could hear Renae's voice in the other room. Ferona's steady tone. And I hated them both for being calm.

A side of me came out that neither of them had seen.

Maybe I hadn't seen it either.

I was angry at the system. At my mother. At life.

At the judge. At the boyfriend. At the trash bags. At every adult who told me this was "for my own good."

At how much I had been expected to carry without ever being asked if I could.

I had followed the rules.

I had stayed quiet.

I had been "resilient."

And I was tired of being resilient.

Maybe it was everything I had held in for too long. Maybe it was just my age catching up to my pain.

Or maybe I was finally realizing that survival isn't the same thing as healing.

I didn't want to be strong.

I wanted my mom.

And that was the part no one knew what to do with.

# WEIGHTLESS MOMENTS, HEAVY TRUTHS

The anger didn't disappear. It stayed under the surface, quiet but present, like a bruise you forget about until someone brushes against it. After that home visit, Renae didn't say much, and I was grateful. She gave me space without making me feel abandoned. A hot meal left on the stove, the TV on in the living room, and my favorite cereal back in the cabinet said, I'm still here.

No speeches. No fixing. Just consistency.

And consistency felt almost suspicious at first.

Life didn't pause. I continued working at the Italian restaurant, saving every tip and paycheck, clocking in, tying on an apron, and having a role that felt safe. I wasn't the foster teen or the girl from the broken home. I was just Irene, the hostess who always showed up, smiled at the regulars, and remembered who liked extra breadsticks.

At work, no one knew my file number.

No one knew about courtrooms or placements.

They just knew I worked hard.

That felt like oxygen.

Saturday mornings became routine. At sunrise, Renae was already mowing the lawn, while I buried my head under a pillow, wondering if she was trying to annoy me. Now I know she was just beating the heat, taking care of her house.

Back then, I was a teenager trying to hold my pain together and still show up for life.

Sometimes I resented how steady she was. How predictable. It felt unfair that she got to be stable when my mother never was.

We were both doing our best.

Sometimes, I caught her watching me. Not with judgment, but with worry. She didn't know how to reach me, but she wasn't ready to stop trying.

I didn't know how to let her.

And that was the truth I didn't say out loud.

I wasn't ready to name what was changing in me. But something was. Between the quiet dinners, the paychecks, the early mornings, and the hum of the lawn mower, I was building a life. Slowly.

Awkwardly.

But part of me kept waiting for it to collapse.

Because good things never lasted.

Not for me.

And for the first time, I was starting to believe I could keep it.

And that belief terrified me more than chaos ever had.

# AGING OUT

Stability had an expiration date.

School was coming to an end. For once, not because I was being moved or pulled out, but because I was finishing my alternative classes: slower-paced, quieter, and filled with students who didn't ask questions. They were people who didn't fit in anywhere else, and for the first time, I fit right where I was. I didn't have to explain myself. I just had to show up and get it done.

No one asked about my past.

No one expected me to be "normal."

We were all carrying something.

That made it easier to breathe.

I was only at the main high school for a few classes. People didn't really ask where I'd been. They glanced at me and moved on, and I learned how to live with that.

Being overlooked used to hurt.

Now it felt like protection.

The school counselor and principal had set up a graduation plan for me. They believed I could do it, and slowly, I started to believe it too. A quiet confidence was settling into my bones, pushing me to finish.

We talked about college.

Me — in college.

It sounded unreal.

College was something stable kids talked about.

Kids with baby pictures in frames and parents in the stands.

Not girls with case files and court dates.

But I wanted more for myself.

I needed more than survival.

Graduation was set for December, right after my eighteenth birthday. I'd officially age out of the system.

Age out.

Such a strange phrase.

Like I was expiring.

Like, protection had a timer.

Because that's what it meant.

No more mandated visits.

No more court oversight.

No more someone legally responsible for making sure I had a bed.

Because I was enrolling in college, I would still receive help transitioning into adulthood. That meant a roof. Support. A chance. Maybe even a future.

But I understood something most eighteen-year-olds didn't.

Support can disappear.

Roofs can vanish.

Adults can change their minds.

It wasn't just about escaping the past anymore.

It was about choosing what came next.

And choosing felt heavier than surviving ever had.

# THE EDGE OF INDEPENDENCE

The state assigned me to a new case manager.

Becca was younger, maybe late twenties. She wore square-framed glasses that slid down her nose when she talked, and her clipboard, covered in color-coded tabs and sticky notes, was always tucked under her arm. Her voice was calm, steady, the kind that didn't rush or overpromise. She wasn't there to save me; she was there to guide me.

No one was saving me anymore. That part was over.

Her job wasn't about where I'd been, but where I was going.

Becca helped me with everything I didn't even know I needed to know — how to budget for groceries, how to pay bills, how to fill out housing paperwork, how to read the fine print adults never warn you about, and how to manage adulthood.

No one had ever taught me how to live without chaos.

And most importantly, how to stay on track. As long as I stayed in school, I would continue receiving support. That was the deal.

And I kept my end of it.

I earned a cheerleading scholarship to Rose State College. I still ask myself how I made it this far, after all the shelters, the group homes, the foster placements, the black trash bags stuffed with my life.

Some girls pack for college. I had been packing to survive since I was ten.

But there I was, in my own apartment just off campus.

I decided to stay in the same town. It felt familiar, safer than starting over again somewhere new. I wanted roots, even if I had to plant them myself.

I became a flyer on the college's co-ed cheer team. It was one of the hardest things I'd ever done, but also one of the most rewarding. Trust. Discipline. Strength.

I was lifted into the air by strangers who eventually became teammates, then friends. I had to believe they wouldn't drop me.

Trusting someone to catch you is different when you've been dropped before.

I had a job with a latchkey program, helping care for elementary kids before and after school. That meant I was up before sunrise, prepping crafts, managing snack time, tying shoes, and wiping tears. Then, racing off to my own classes. By late afternoon, I was back again, signing kids out to their parents with a tired smile.

I didn't complain. I was grateful.

Grateful felt safer than exhausted.

It paid the bills. And it felt good to be someone little ones could count on.

I was doing it. Learning how to stand on my own feet while the state stood behind me. They offered help: housing support, tuition assistance, and monthly check-ins from Becca.

But none of it came with a guidebook.

No one tells you how to be an adult when you skipped being a child.

And I was not perfect.

But I was trying.

And in the middle of building a life, I did something big.

I opened the door to my past.

I let my mom back in.

We didn't plan it. It just happened. A few texts. Then a visit.

She was working as a waitress, living in an apartment with little furniture or belongings. She had her own battles, her own pace.

We didn't talk about what happened, where I'd been, or what I'd lost.

Maybe that was for the best. Maybe silence was the only common ground we had. Or maybe we were both too afraid to touch the truth.

But I was there.

And she opened the door.

And I walked in anyway.

## QUIET SHIFTS

My mom and I saw each other every few weeks. It wasn't consistent, but it was okay. We were rebuilding something slowly, on our own terms, in small pieces. We didn't talk much about the past, or about where I'd been.

Maybe that was for the best.

Or maybe silence was the only way we knew how to survive each other.

She told me about a man she'd met at the restaurant, a regular who came in often. He worked on computers. He didn't drink, or if he did, it was just a glass of wine now and then. He had a son. A house.

Eventually, she moved in with him. And she stopped drinking.

There was no big reunion or emotional breakthrough, but she was trying, and I could see it. She looked different, not just in the way she dressed and carried herself, but in her eyes. The chaos that used to live there had settled a little.

Settled is not the same as gone. I knew that.

I didn't know how long it would last, and I didn't let myself lean all the way into it. But I noticed.

We were both learning how to live different lives.

I came to her house for dinner. Nothing fancy, just something warm and shared. Sometimes she made spaghetti or a casserole. The TV hummed low in the background, and we sat across from each other, talking about work, school, cheer. Not the past.

We were learning each other all over again.

Carefully. Like touching something fragile.

She came to some of my college basketball games and watched me cheer. I'd scan the crowd before we started, and when I saw her there, clapping or smiling, something inside me relaxed.

She showed up.

And that meant something.

Those moments felt normal, like we'd skipped all the chaos and landed on our feet. Like the pain had been a long, confusing dream.

I wanted to believe the worst of us was behind us.

She was trying. I was trying.

Her boyfriend was funny, quirky in a harmless way. Always ready with a random fact or strange joke. And he could cook. Not microwave meals, but real food. Stir-fry. Grilled chicken with roasted vegetables. Meals that required intention.

He brought out a side of my mom I'd never really seen before.

They laughed together. I hadn't realized how long it had been since I'd heard her laughter without tension underneath it.

She wasn't perfect, and neither was I. For the first time in a long time, we weren't surviving each other. We were existing side by side.

Trying to move forward, not backward.

And that was enough for now.

My body had been keeping score long before my knee gave out.

Cheer gave me structure, purpose, something to fight for. But it demanded everything in return. During my time at Rose State College, we traveled to the NCA Nationals in Daytona, Florida. Between performances, we practiced stunts on the sand, barefoot, pushing through repetition like we always did.

That's where it happened.

One wrong landing. A sharp twist I felt immediately.

I knew before I hit the ground that something had shifted in more than just my knee.

The first surgery came soon after. I tried to return before my body was ready, afraid of losing my place. Afraid of losing myself.

I went back to stunting. Back to training. And I re-injured the same knee.

Recovery stretched on. Quiet. Lonely. Mostly alone in my apartment. Icing. Bracing. Hoping it would finally hold.

After my second surgery, I needed help.

I didn't plan on staying long, but I moved in with my mom for a while. Being there felt okay. Safe, even.

I'd withdrawn from my college classes. I could no longer cheer. Without school and cheer, the support I was receiving from the state disappeared, too.

Everything that once kept me afloat — my schedule, my income, my structure — vanished.

When the cheering stopped, so did the scaffolding holding my life upright.

I didn't have many options. And she offered.

So I stayed.

It was like she was making up for lost time. She cooked for me. Real meals. The kind I hadn't had when I lived with her before. Warm. Filling. Thoughtful. She washed my clothes. Made sure I had my medications. Checked on me more than once during the day.

I didn't have to ask. She just did it.

She showed up. And that presence was everything.

For a while, it felt like healing. Like maybe we had outrun the old ghosts. Maybe this softer, steadier version of her was here to stay.

But healing built on silence has cracks you cannot see at first.

Little shifts began to happen.

She'd snap, quick and sharp, over something small. I'd forget to take the trash out. Leave a dish in the sink. And suddenly I was "ungrateful" for living rent-free under her roof.

The word ungrateful landed harder than it should have.

I was recovering from surgery. Trying to figure out who I was without cheer. Without structure. Without the state safety net. Trying to decide what came next. Trying not to collapse under the weight of it.

But I didn't always feel like a daughter.

Sometimes I felt like a burden.

A guest.

A debt.

And I was thankful. I said thank you. But those words started to feel invisible.

Gratitude became currency. And I was terrified of running out.

The familiar feeling returned. The one that sits low in your stomach and tightens slowly. The one that whispers, don't get too comfortable.

Still, I stayed.

Because there was love there, too.

And love — even complicated, unpredictable love — was worth holding onto.

Even when it cost me something to hold it.

# WHEN HOPE COLLIDES

Summer break arrived, and I felt like myself again. I had a plan... at least the beginning of one. I wasn't frozen anymore. I applied to a dental program and was saving up for a trip with Marie.

We were teenagers. Not perfect. But full of hope.

I was always on the go, and my mom didn't like it. She said I was never home. That I was ungrateful.

I didn't know if her reaction was normal or not.

Was it typical for a parent to be upset when their daughter was busy working, planning for the future, and trying to live?

Or was this what love looked like when it was afraid of being left behind?

I'd never had a mom like that before. A mom who cooked dinner and asked where I was going. A mom who wanted to sit and talk.

And part of me didn't know how to belong in something steady.

I was doing the best I could, showing up for life. I'd earned a scholarship. Enrolled in school. Worked hard. I was building something new with my mom.

But every time she called me ungrateful, something old flinched inside me.

One night, her frustration started before I even made it to the dinner table. Her words hit like jabs, one after the other. Something about my attitude. About being home. About not appreciating what I had.

The room felt smaller. The air thicker. Like I was fourteen again instead of grown.

I sat in silence until I couldn't anymore.

And then I snapped.

"SCREW IT!"

The words exploded out of me, louder than I meant. Louder than I could take back.

I couldn't take one more hit.

I wasn't just reacting to that night. I was reacting to years.

It wasn't who I wanted to be. But I cracked.

I was trying so hard to make everything work. And still, it wasn't enough.

I was tired of being grateful for crumbs and calling it a feast.

Maybe it was just who we were. Maybe all that hope was too fragile to hold up against the weight of everything we'd been through.

I grabbed what I could carry and walked out.

No plan. No backup.

Just me... and my car.

And the familiar ache of leaving before I could be left.

That night, I slept in it.

Then the next night. And the next.

I parked in neighborhoods that felt safe. Sat under streetlights that flickered overhead.

I locked the doors twice. Then checked them again.

And wondered how I'd gotten here again.

It wasn't new. Not really. I'd done this before when my mom and I left places in the middle of the night. Bags packed fast. No clear plan. Just survival.

But this time, I wasn't a child being led away.

I'd walked out on my own.

I had my own car. My own life. My own job.

And still, I felt like a child pretending to be strong.

I needed space.

Not just from the yelling. Not just from the dinner table tension.

But from the ache that had been building.

The floodgates of the past had cracked open. Years of silence. Starting over. Stuffing down the things I couldn't fix.

I wasn't angry about one argument.

I was angry that stability still felt temporary.

I sat behind the wheel, legs pulled to my chest, trying to make sense of what I was feeling.

Part of me wanted her to come looking for me. Part of me didn't want to be found.

I didn't call anyone.

I needed to know what this was first.

Was it just a bad night? A cooling-off period?

Or was this another breaking point in a long line?

For a few nights, I bounced between sleeping in my car and crashing on a friend's couch.

I didn't talk about it much. Didn't explain.

I kept the details tucked away.

Because if I said it out loud, "I'm sleeping in my car again," it would mean I hadn't escaped anything at all.

Most people didn't know the full weight of the life I carried before they met me.

And I wasn't ready to open that box again.

Eventually, I went back to my mom's house.

We didn't talk about what happened.

We just kept going.

But it wasn't forgotten.

It stayed with me.

Not just for the pain.

But for the way I handled it.

I didn't spiral. I didn't disappear.

I held on to myself... even when it hurt.

But holding on came at a cost.

Every time I chose love, I had to choose it knowing it might not hold.

Maybe that meant I was growing.

We tried to smooth it over. To pretend the sharp edges had dulled. For a little while, we slipped back into routine. Dinner. Work. Polite conversation.

But something in me had shifted. I couldn't un-feel what those nights in my car had shown me. I didn't want to run every time things got hard. But I also didn't want to keep living somewhere love felt conditional.

The second time I left, it wasn't loud. It wasn't dramatic. I packed quietly. With a plan.

And this time, I didn't come back.

# WIDE OPEN ROADS

For the first time in my life, I wasn't under the state's watch. And I wasn't under my mom's roof either.

I had chosen to stand on my own.

There were rough days. Couch hopping. Quiet setbacks. Uncertainty that sat heavy some mornings.

But I kept showing up. Kept trying.

No one was monitoring me anymore. No one was checking in to see if I'd made it home.

No one would come looking if I unraveled.

Freedom is beautiful, but it is also very quiet.

The dental assisting program pushed me, but I pushed back. I stayed up late studying. Practiced procedures in the mirror. Showed up on the days when doubt whispered I didn't belong.

Doubt sounds loud when you've spent years being temporary.

Testing season was around the corner, and the nerves were real.

I leaned into my friendship with one of the girls in the

program. We became close. Studying late. Laughing when our brains hit overload. Dreaming about what came next.

She was hired first at an orthodontist's office not far from where we'd studied. I was proud of her.

A few weeks later, I got the call too.

Same office. Same scrubs. Same next chapter.

That job became more than work.

It was proof. Proof that I could start somewhere and not be asked to leave.

Proof that I could earn something and keep it.

Then came my first apartment.

Small. Simple. Mine.

My name was on the lease.

My name. Not the state's. Not a foster placement. Not temporary paperwork.

My dishes were in the cabinet. And peace, in every corner.

There were no check-ins. No rules taped to the fridge. No one listening for arguments through thin walls.

Just quiet.

The kind that settles in after a storm and makes you realize how loud your life used to be.

I picked out a shower curtain I actually liked. Learned how quickly laundry piles up. Budgeted every grocery run down to the last dollar.

And I loved it.

Even the hard parts.

Because struggle feels different when it's chosen.

My mom and I stayed connected, but not under the same roof.

And that was better for us.

Healthier.

We had Sunday dinners. The occasional lunch. A text now and then:

You okay

It wasn't perfect.

But it wasn't chaos either.

And sometimes that felt like a miracle.

One night, I was sitting on the floor of my apartment, folding laundry. The TV buzzing softly in the background. Leftovers still warm on the counter.

And it hit me.

This was my life.

Not a placement. Not a shelter. Not someone else's rules.

Mine.

No one could pack it into a trash bag and leave it on a porch.

I wasn't just surviving anymore.

I was living. Choosing. Becoming.

This chapter was mine.

Life picked up pace. I worked. Tried to keep up with everything adulthood demanded.

But I also made space for lightness.

On weekends, I went to tailgate parties with friends. In the Midwest, football wasn't just a sport; it was a season. Something to gather around.

We'd pile into cars. Drive an hour out of town. Meet up with old friends or friends of friends.

Sometimes we didn't even care who was playing.

I liked the noise. The crowds. The feeling of being just another girl in a team shirt, not the girl with a story.

I didn't really date close to home.

Maybe I was protecting myself.

Maybe I was complicated.

Maybe I was both.

I couldn't easily hand my story to someone new. And it was hard for me to trust.

When you grow up with cracks in your foundation, you learn to test the ground before stepping.

People said one thing but meant another.

Promises were made, then broken.

Love had always come with conditions.

Behave.

Be grateful.

Don't be too much.

Don't leave.

Don't need too much.

I didn't know yet what unconditional looked like.

I kept things light. Fun. Safe.

But sometimes, late at night, after the laughter faded and the makeup came off, I'd sit on the edge of my bed and wonder what it would be like to let someone in.

Not the polished version of me.

The whole one.

The girl who packed her life in trash bags.

The girl who learned how to leave first.

The girl who didn't always believe she'd be chosen.

How do you know if someone is who they say they are?

How do you believe they'll stay when so many others haven't?

How do you rest in love when your nervous system still expects the door to close?

I didn't have the answers.

But I was asking the questions.

And maybe that was a start.

## YOUNG ENOUGH TO LEAP

Stability was supposed to feel like enough. It didn't.

Because stability is safety. And I had spent my whole life surviving. I didn't know how to just be safe. I wanted to feel alive.

I was doing well. Really well. A job in orthodontics, my own place, steady routines.

On paper, it looked like I had it together. But I was still young. Still aching to live freely. And I felt I'd missed out on everything while surviving my way through life.

"Greece," Marie said with a grin.

A trip. An adventure. A break from routines we were both still getting used to. I had a steady job. Bills. Responsibilities.

But I said yes anyway.

Maybe it was reckless, but I quit my job.

Or maybe I was tired of proving I could be responsible.

I had spent my whole life being careful.

I wanted one decision that felt wild and entirely mine.

I hadn't come that far to play safe. I was young, and I wanted to live like it — unbound, even for a moment.

I packed a bag, clutched my passport, and reminded myself that not all lessons are learned in classrooms. Some are learned by leaping.

We landed in Kypseli, Athens, exhausted but buzzing with excitement. Everything felt new, ancient, and alive. We were just two girls from the Midwest chasing a dream. We explored Athens, wandered winding streets, and stood beneath the towering Acropolis.

The girl who had slept in her car.

The girl whose life once fit into black trash bags.

The girl who had stood in courtrooms while adults decided her future.

She was standing under the Acropolis.

How was this even possible? Was it because I never looked back? Because I had to survive? Had foster care given me the space to become this girl who bought her own plane ticket and worked extra jobs?

I'd earned every step that brought me there.

We didn't speak a lick of Greek, but Marie, dying of thirst, walked up to a small café and ordered a bottle of water. What she didn't know was that it usually came sparkling. She opened it, took a big gulp… and promptly spit it out everywhere.

"What is this?" she gasped.

The poor man blinked at us.

"You said 'water' in a… very interesting accent."

We laughed until our stomachs hurt.

Still thirsty and determined, Marie spotted a calm stone fountain. The water looked clean enough. So she poured out the sparkling stuff, dipped her bottle in, and started drinking.

Huge mistake.

She had just stolen holy water.

Suddenly, people were shouting, pointing, chasing us like we were wild Americans. Which we kind of were. We ran, laughing and breathless, hearts pounding, adrenaline surging, until we reached the steps of the Acropolis and the world was quiet again.

No one was yelling at us for real.

No one was threatening to leave.

No one was slamming doors.

We were just two girls who made a mistake.

And that felt new.

We caught our breath, turned to face the city, and let the ancient marble remind us that we'd made it. Two girls with too many stories, too many bruises, and still — so much wonder.

After Athens, we traveled to a small village near the Mediterranean Sea. Marie passed out on my shoulder somewhere in the middle of nowhere, and soon I drifted off too.

We woke up in another world.

White and blue homes stacked like blocks. Creaking doors. Smiling windows.

We stayed with a local family in a three-story house with a small store on the ground floor. The older kids slept on the top level, where a balcony overlooked the village.

It was beautiful. Quiet. Humble. Real.

The family welcomed us with open arms and warm smiles. When the mother leaned in for the customary greeting, I panicked and accidentally kissed her on the lips.

My whole body turned red.

Then laughter. Hers. The dad's. The kids'. It filled the room like music. No one was offended, just amused.

Dinner was waiting. Olives. Cheese. Warm bread. Fish pulled from the sea that day.

That night, on the third floor beside my friend, with a full stomach and the sound of waves drifting through the window, I didn't feel like a guest in my own life.

For once, I wasn't waiting for someone to tell me I didn't belong.

We woke to the smell of coffee and sunlight already warming the air. We settled into the village rhythm — work in the mornings, long lunches, naps, and shops reopening when the heat softened.

Marie and I leaned into it. Lazy afternoons on the beach, salty wind in our hair, toes buried in sand.

One afternoon at a beachside café, someone handed us Ouzo. Clear. Icy. Tasting like black licorice. No one warned us how strong it was.

The sun felt heavier after that. The laughter came easier. The edges of the day softened.

I had chased numbness before. This felt different.

This felt chosen.

We stumbled back to the house, sandals dangling from our hands, skin warm, and fell into our first real Greek nap.

That night, the older kids took us into the square. Outdoor tables. Warm yellow lights. Music filling the air. They taught us how to order in Greek, clapping when we got it close enough.

People danced in circles under the stars.

It wasn't a performance. It was belonging.

Marie and I joined in, tripping and laughing, completely comfortable in our own skin.

Later, we ate warm sandwiches stuffed with meat, sauce, and French fries inside the bread. We stood on the street corner devouring them like they were sacred.

It was the best sandwich I've ever had.

That trip was more than a vacation.

It was proof.

Proof that I was not just the girl with the file. Not just the girl who left first. Not just the girl who survived.

But a girl who could leap.

Maybe healing isn't quiet.

Maybe sometimes it looks like dancing too hard.

Laughing too loud.

Quitting the safe job.

Booking the ticket anyway.

Trusting that you are allowed to take up space in a world that once tried to contain you.

Halfway across the world, dancing under foreign stars, I felt light.

Untamed.

Possible.

And for the first time in a long time, I wasn't bracing for something to fall apart.

I was living.

# THE QUESTION I WASN'T READY FOR

Coming home from Greece felt like landing back in reality with a soft thud. Not a crash. Not a spiral. Just the quiet return to gravity.

Bills. Searching for work. Responsibility. The weight of what comes next.

The sun still rose the same way it always had, but I felt different under it. Less desperate. More awake.

I tried to slip back into the groove. Early mornings. Routines. Figuring out life one step at a time. The rhythm helped. It always had.

I applied for a new job at a general dentistry office. A fresh environment. A clean slate. Another chance to prove — mostly to myself — that I could keep building forward.

My interview with Dr. Stalder started off well. Polite conversation. Smiles. Confidence I had practiced in the mirror.

Then he asked,

"Where do you see yourself in ten years?"

It felt like the air had been sucked out of the room.

Ten years.

Ten years ago, I did not know where I would sleep.

Ten years ago, adults decided my future in courtrooms.

Ten years ago, survival was the only timeline I understood.

I had never thought that far ahead.

When you grow up surviving, you do not plan. You react. You make it through the day. Handle the next fire. Learn how to adjust when the ground shifts beneath you.

You do not imagine a decade down the road.

Imagining stability felt dangerous.

Like if I named it, it would disappear.

That kind of hope had always felt fragile. Too out of reach.

I fumbled through something generic. Said what I thought I was supposed to say. Smiled. Nodded.

I spoke in safe answers.

Not honest ones.

I knew it was not enough.

I walked out of that office holding back tears, already replaying that moment, already rewriting answers in my head that I had not been brave enough to give out loud.

I crawled into bed and pulled the blanket over my head.

What if this was it?

What if I was still the girl who could survive anything but could not picture a future?

The doubt crept in fast, whispering old lies in a new voice.

A few days passed. I kept moving. Running errands. Answering emails. Pretending the question had not lodged itself deep in my chest.

But it stayed with me.

One evening, I went to my mom's for dinner and brought her a small jar of seashells and sand from Greece.

She smiled when I handed it to her, turning it slowly in her hands like it held more than just pieces of the sea.

Maybe it did.

Maybe it was proof that distance did not always mean disappearance. That we were still building something, even if it did not look like anyone else's version of normal.

That night, I went to bed lighter. Still uncertain, but not sinking.

The next morning, my phone rang after I had already hit the snooze button three times. My voice was thick with sleep as I cleared my throat and tried to sound awake.

It was the dental office.

I sat straight up in bed.

The voice on the other end was cheerful. "We'd love to offer you the position. When can you start?"

"Really?"

"Really. We will train you. When can you start?"

Monday?

"Yes. We will see you then."

I thanked them, hung up, and just sat there for a second, phone still warm in my hand.

They had seen something in me. Even when I could not see it in myself.

I was not just a girl trying to prove she deserved a seat at the table.

I was becoming someone who didn't have to earn her place anymore.

That day, I let myself picture ten years from now.

Not the full picture. Not the house. Not the partner. Not the exact path.

Just one simple truth.

I would still be standing.

And this time, by choice.

I took a long shower, letting the water rinse off the doubt and the fear that I was always one step behind.

On Monday, I walked into the office with nervous energy

tucked beneath my scrubs. Everything felt new. Sterile. Bright. The kind of place where people trusted you with their smiles.

Dr. Stalder greeted me with the same calm professionalism. His staff welcomed me like they had already decided I belonged.

Training was intense. New routines. Tools. Procedures.

I kept a small notepad in my pocket, afraid to miss something important. I asked questions. Listened harder than I ever had in school.

Not because I had to. But because I wanted to.

I was not just working to survive anymore.

I was building something I cared about.

After my shift, I drove home with the windows down, music low, a tired but satisfied hum settling into my body. I changed out of my scrubs, heated up leftovers, and stood quietly in my kitchen, breathing in the stillness of a life that didn't feel temporary.

It was the kind of quiet I used to ache for when I was bouncing from home to home.

Some nights, I caught myself smiling while folding laundry or brushing my teeth. Small moments that felt earned. Like my body finally trusted that nothing bad was about to happen.

I still did not have all the answers.

But I had a job. A purpose. A future that felt open instead of threatening.

I did not have a ten-year plan.

But I had today.

And that was enough to keep going. To take the next right step. To quiet the old voices that said I could not do this.

I used to think survival was the goal. Just making it through.

But I was beginning to understand something else.

Life could be more than that.

There was still healing ahead. Still fears I had not named.

But this job, this routine, this small, steady world was not just a place to land.

It was a place to grow.

I was not waiting for the other shoe to drop anymore.

I was lacing both of them up.

And walking forward.

# OFF THE ICE, INTO SOMETHING NEW

Life didn't change all at once. It tilted. Not a collapse. Not a storm. Just a shift I could feel beneath my feet.

I called my mom about the Ice Girls audition.

She said, "Go for it."

I had already decided. But hearing her support steadied something in me. For so many years, I had learned to move without asking. It felt strange to be encouraged instead of warned.

I sent in a screenshot of myself and a short bio. They would choose from the submissions and call the girls they wanted for in-person interviews.

A few days later, my phone rang.

I got the interview, and it went well.

When they asked if I knew how to skate, I said yes. I had taught myself as a kid.

"Do you know anything about hockey?"

"Um… not really. I know they fight."

Did that seriously just come out of my mouth?

Somehow, I survived the interview and performed my

routine flawlessly. They thanked me and said they would let me know within forty-eight hours.

Then they called.

I made it.

I was working full-time at the dental office, and I was an official American Hockey League Ice Girl. I worked during the day, practiced in the evenings, showed up for events, and cheered at home games.

It was decent money.

And a lot of fun.

Hockey is fast and chaotic, but I liked the energy. The noise. The speed. The way the crowd held its breath and then exploded. It felt alive.

And I liked being part of something loud on purpose. Not loud because it was breaking. Loud because it was a celebration.

My friends came to some games and cheered me on.

One night, when I walked out of the locker room, I saw a guy in a brown suit standing nearby.

He looked out of place in what they call the tunnel. Tall. Solid. Like he belonged on the ice instead of beside it. Even out of gear, hockey players always seemed enormous to me — all shoulders and presence.

But this one stood out.

Dirty blond hair. Strong features that looked carved rather than soft. Blue eyes. Sharp. Curious. A darker goatee that made him look older than he probably was.

"Are you guys the new draft picks?"

I had no idea what he meant.

My teammate and I just looked at each other.

I could barely make eye contact.

Not nervous.

Not shy.

Alert.

Like my body had noticed something before my mind could explain it.

We were not supposed to talk to the hockey players. Some of the girls did. I tried not to.

Two weekends later, the team was out of town, and I finally had a moment to breathe.

A random number popped up on my phone.

"How are you?"

"Um… who is this?"

"Shaun."

"I'm sorry, I don't know any Shauns."

"One of your friends gave me your number."

Oh.

Oh no.

Brown Suit.

"Oh, hey, Brown Suit."

"It's tan, actually."

"Couldn't tell."

"You might be color blind."

We went back and forth like that for a while. Easy. Quick. Unexpectedly funny.

He asked me out.

I didn't soften it.

"I don't date athletes."

Three dots appeared. Disappeared. Then another message.

What about your friend? The one who was standing with you that night.

I laughed out loud.

Alone.

I sent him her number.

"Good luck."

A few days later, he texted again.

"Okay, I get why you said good luck. Definitely not my speed."

"Didn't think so."

"Then why give me her number?"

"Because you asked."

"Why didn't you warn me?"

"I did. I said good luck."

There was a pause.

Then: "Can I take you out?"

"No."

After a game, he offered to walk me to my car.

I said no.

This continued for weeks.

He would check in. Show up. Stay consistent.

Not loud. Not pushy.

Just there.

And that was new.

Most people in my life had been intense or absent.

Too much. Or gone.

He did not chase. He did not retreat.

He just stayed.

Eventually, I agreed to meet him. I warned him I would be coming straight from work. In scrubs. No makeup. Hair in a bun.

"I'll look terrible."

He did not care.

I walked into his apartment and immediately noticed how tall he was. I am 5'3". He had to be at least 6'4".

His place was clean. Candles lit. Music playing. Simple. Shoes neatly by the door.

"You can take your shoes off," he said.

"No, thank you."

He gave me a look, but my toenails were jacked up.

I sat on the opposite side of the couch. Nerves through the roof.

Please do not try to kiss me. I will die.

"You don't have to sit so far away."

"I'm good, thanks."

He asked what shows I watched.

"I don't watch TV."

"What? Are you human?"

"I just work a lot."

That seemed to stump him.

Then my phone rang.

It was Stephanie.

"Hey, are you still coming?"

"Yeah, I'll be there soon."

"Where are you going?" Shaun asked.

"I told you, I work more than one job. I'm a personal trainer too."

He did not seem thrilled, but he did not stop me.

"I'll walk you out."

"No, it's okay."

"I'm walking you out."

We walked to the door. I gave him a side hug.

He looked confused.

But he hugged me back and said, "I'll see you later."

And for the first time in a long time, I hoped someone meant it.

Because I had learned to leave before anyone else could. But I had never learned how to stay.

And maybe this time, I wanted to try.

# LEARNING TO STAY

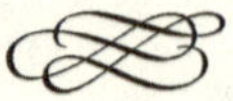

I didn't expect to see him again after that night. Not because anything went wrong, but because that's what life had trained me to expect.

People didn't stay. Interest faded. Energy shifted.

At twenty-four, maybe for the first time, someone had shown up without trying to take anything from me. And that alone felt suspicious.

Maybe I had said too much.

Maybe I had been too quiet.

Maybe I had made it complicated, the way I always seemed to. I had never learned how to let something be simple.

A few days later, Shaun texted.

"How's the toothpaste scented life?"

I laughed, remembering the first time I had gone to his apartment. The way he leaned back, smiled, and told me I smelled like toothpaste. It wasn't flirtation the way I was used to. It was familiar. Easy.

It started small. Texting here and there. Sharing songs. Pictures. Little pieces of our days. Slowly, the tone shifted. He didn't rush me. He didn't ask for more than I was ready to give.

He didn't disappear either.

He was just there. Steady. And steady felt foreign.

Foreign enough that I kept waiting for the catch.

We started seeing each other more. Sometimes dinner. Sometimes just sitting in his apartment talking. No pressure. No performance. No guessing where I stood.

He made space for my awkwardness. For my hesitation.

Once, after a long shift, I showed up exhausted. Still in scrubs, hair pulled back, running on fumes. He didn't comment on how I looked. He didn't ask what was wrong. He handed me a glass of water, turned the TV down, and asked,

"You want quiet or company?"

No one had ever asked me that before.

It wasn't dramatic. It was slow. Careful. Almost quiet.

But quiet had never meant safe in my life before. Quiet used to mean something was about to explode.

He asked questions no one had ever bothered to ask. Not just favorite food or favorite movie, but the ones underneath. My family. My fears. What I thought love looked like. What I was afraid of losing.

At first, I answered cautiously. I had spent years curating what parts of my story people were allowed to hold. If you control the narrative, you control the damage.

But he didn't flinch. He didn't pity me. He didn't try to fix me. He didn't treat me like something fragile.

He just listened.

And something in me softened in a way I had not planned. Soft felt dangerous. Soft meant you could be hurt.

I had spent so much of my life preparing for exits. Watching tone shifts. Reading between the lines. Bracing for disappointment before it had a chance to land.

But he kept showing up.

There were moments my instinct was to pull back. To sabotage it before he could. That old reflex whispered, Leave first. Because if you leave first, you don't have to watch someone else do it.

But he didn't chase. He didn't withdraw. He just stayed.

And staying did not feel like a trap. It felt different. It felt earned.

I didn't know what we were. I didn't know where it was headed.

But for the first time, I wasn't calculating an escape route. I wasn't rehearsing goodbye.

I was present.

And that felt more terrifying than any breakup ever could.

Because this time, the risk wasn't being left. The risk was letting myself believe someone might stay. And choosing to stay, too.

Not because I needed to be saved.

But because I wanted to be seen.

# EPILOGUE — WHAT COMES NEXT

One door closes, and just beyond it, another quietly swings open.

I used to think survival was the whole story, that making it through was the victory. But standing here now, I understand something I couldn't see before. Survival was only the beginning.

There is more ahead. More lessons that will stretch me. More love that will ask me to trust again. More unexpected turns, some that will break my heart, some that will carry me across oceans, some that will change everything I thought I knew about partnership, patience, and faith.

In the next chapter of my life, I will learn what it means to build something lasting with another person. To love someone whose world moves fast. Whose dreams pull us into unfamiliar places. Whose career will test everything I thought I understood about stability.

I will learn what trust looks like when the past still whispers. What commitment requires when life refuses to slow down. What it means to stay, even when leaving would feel easier.

I will keep growing, sometimes gracefully, sometimes clumsily, sometimes undoing parts of myself I once believed were permanent.

Healing, I've learned, is not a destination. It is a practice. It is waking up and choosing again. It is believing that the girl who survived deserved more than endurance.

Thank you for walking this road with me, for witnessing the messy, uneven, beautiful work of becoming. For seeing the girl who carried her life in trash bags and believing she was always meant to become this woman.

The story is not over.

It never was.

Survival built the foundation. But love, risk, faith, and courage will build the rest.

Like the first light after a long night, the future holds promises I am only beginning to understand.

And this time, I am not bracing for impact.

I am stepping forward.

Ready.

# ACKNOWLEDGMENTS

To the people who showed up in the moments that mattered, thank you. Some of you offered a place to stay, a ride, a meal, or a quiet space when the world felt too heavy. You may never know how much those small acts held me together.

To the teachers, counselors, and adults who saw something in me when I could not see it in myself, thank you for giving me steadiness during years when I had very little of it.

To the friends who became family, thank you for the laughter, the honesty, and the reminders that I was not as alone as I felt. Your presence shaped more of my life than you realize.

To Stephanie, thank you for being one of the first people who made me feel safe. Your presence in my my life changed more than you will ever know.

To my husband Colten, thank you for your patience, your steadiness, and the quiet way you made room for me to grow. You helped me understand what safety feels like, and that changed everything.

To the girl I used to be, thank you for surviving long enough for me to write this. You carried more than you should have, and you kept going anyway. To the woman I am now, thank you for choosing healing, even when it felt unfamiliar.

And to every reader who picked up this book and held my story with care, thank you. Your willingness to witness these pages means more than you know.

# ABOUT THE AUTHOR

Ashley Irene is a special education teacher, writer, and advocate whose work explores resilience, survival, and the lifelong search for belonging. Her first memoir traces her journey through foster care, instability, and the fight to build a life rooted in safety, identity, and love.

Today, Ashley lives in Virginia with her husband Colten and their two children. Her family's story includes both triumphs and challenges, from raising a neurodivergent child and navigating medical setbacks to discovering her biological father through DNA discovery. These experiences continue to shape her voice as a mother, teacher, and writer.

Ashley holds a Bachelor's degree in Health Science and a Master's degree in Special Education. She is currently writing her second book, which follows her journey from meeting Shaun as a professional hockey player to marriage, motherhood, and the years spent traveling for his career — including their time living in Germany — and the unexpected turns that strengthened her family.

www.ingramcontent.com/pod-product-compliance
Lightning Source LLC
LaVergne TN
LVHW090524110826
845146LV00003B/972